Contents

Introduction	1
Wisdom and Wealth: The Catalyst of Transformation	10
Who Are You?	20
To What Purpose Do We Exist?	41
How Should We Act Towards One Another?	62
How to Apply the Knowledge?	77
Final Thoughts	89
Notes	92
Bibliography	106
Appendix One: Social Justice	110
Appendix Two: "Rethinking Prosperity…"	121

As a starting point, the program of education must be based on a clear vision of the kind of society that we wish to live in; and the kind of individuals that will bring this about. It needs to help learners reflect on the purpose of life and help them to step out of their cultural realities to develop alternative visions and approaches to the problems at hand and to understand the manifold consequences of their behaviors and to adjust these accordingly.

Schools themselves must become participants in the social transformation processes. The curriculum cannot simply aim to impart relevant knowledge and skills; rather it should aim to develop the vast potential inherent in the human being. Individuals must be assisted to channel this potential towards the betterment of their communities and the advancement of society as a whole. The level of consciousness and the deep spirit of service and collaboration required to transform individual behaviors and institutional forces in the direction of sustainability will require a transformation of educational processes commensurate with the task at hand.

(Bahá'í International Community, *Rethinking Prosperity*)

Introduction

The fundamentals of the whole economic condition are divine in nature and are associated with the world of the heart and spirit. This is fully explained in the Baha'i teaching, and without knowledge of its principles no improvement in the economic state can be realized...When the love of God is established, everything else will be realized. This is the true foundation of all economics.

('Abdu'l-Baha, *The Promulgation of Universal Peace*: 238)

We live in a time of chaos and confusion, despair and degradation, and people everywhere search desperately for a way out of a darkening horizon. Of course, this is not new in any absolute sense. People have lived through numerous such times. What is new is that upheaval is everywhere. Humanity itself is threatened. We are not just experiencing cultural exhaustion, massive civil unrest, or yet another crisis of government or economy, depending upon what land or people one is observing. We are not just at the end of an era or even an age, but of an entire order of human life and thought.

A new way of looking at our selves and the world is necessary; a new light is required to shine within human beings that enables us to see and formulate new answers—perhaps even new kinds of answers—to urgent questions that cannot be answered in the usual way.

Changing our view of human nature changes our understanding of everything else. This internal paradigm-shift is difficult for many reasons, chief of which is, in my view, the misinformation we receive about ourselves. We are victims of what Bahá'u'lláh calls "lack of a proper education". [1] There is always a connection between social crisis and new moral possibility. Yet full response-ability cannot be achieved when one suffers under the burden of a puny form of belief in oneself or in higher and greater spiritual powers. Because of an improper education, we believe our humanity is something less, much less, than it really is. We say things like "We are only human", because we want to rationalize or excuse a sorry piece of thought or stupid bit of behavior. But we also say it because we don't know or no longer remember that a human being is the most powerful, wonderful, and noble creature in the cosmos. We can't hear our inner voices, put no faith in our imagination, are no longer fired by the sacred longings of the human spirit. We are without vision, and are left with only dreams.

Solving our most intractable problems starts, I feel, with a new vision of humanity. The Book of Proverbs puts this truth well: "Where there is no vision, the people perish." [2] Vision, then, is at least as important as bread, but fear and wrong conditioning delays understanding of this truth. No doubt vision without the means to implement it is just fine words and wonderful pictures. Too great a gap between possibility and "reality" often ends in frustration and despair. But, too, means without vision are destined for only short-sighted pragmatic goals. A great vision fires the imagination which taps the energies of motivation which, in turn, generates the means to execute the vision. This means a transfer of energy from pragmatic to idealistic purposes. Where to find such a vision? I find it in the Bahá'í Teachings. The Universal House of Justice writes that the guidance that the Bahá'í teachings offer "does not comprise a series of specific answers to current problems, but rather the illumination of an entirely new way of life. Without this way of life the problems are insoluble; with it they will either not arise or, if they arise, can be resolved." [3]

This essay explores some implications resident within the two-paragraph opening quote on education as these relate to improving the economics of life. (The full statement is

Appendix Two.) It is not, then, concerned in any way with overhauling the political machinery of state, or shoring up the weakened institutions of civil society, or with fixing the structural inequalities of opportunity in the economy. It advocates no political action, puts forth no social platforms, and suggests no economic policies for creating jobs or innovations in either the relations of production or the institutional distribution of wealth. Neither is it yet another manifesto of artistic and cultural renewal, nor an anxious call to return to the foundations of any religious tradition.

The view presented is that of ideal education for an ideal community. It is a vision of people creating prosperity, using spiritual virtues as currency. Hence there are no personal investment strategies and not even a side glance at topics like individual financial planning. Neither will the reader find stock market tips or the steps to be a millionaire by saving $10.00 a day. It is concerned only with the spiritual state of human beings, both individual and in small groups, and with identifying the advance guard of a new community. The people in this vision do not yet exist in any significant numbers, though their numbers increase daily. But the vision includes every human being on the planet. It is a vision of our true selves acting in real ways, though this may not be recognized by many.

That's because, economically, applying a vision of real humanity focuses not on economics, but, rather, on a larger idea, prosperity. Modern economics is those principles and practices that have to do with producing, distributing and consuming material wealth, goods and services. The more of these one has, consumes or produces, the richer one supposedly is. Yet even the colossally affluent among us vaguely sense that something is really wrong with that equation. Prosperity includes material plenty, of course. Without plenty, prosperity is a pipe-dream of impracticality. Prosperity is based on the shared sense of spiritual well-being and connection that flows from belonging to a community of mutual care. True prosperity will never be achieved by setting our sights solely upon gaining ever more material wealth, for reasons that will become clear. Hence, though wealth obviously plays an essential role in achieving prosperity, I believe that it is human and moral relations of care that are the key to prosperity and that point the way out of our malaise.

In this sense, the essay is a throwback. Prior to our modern materialist mania—i.e. from Aristotle till about the sixteenth century when the Catholic Church lost its moral hold on European society and that ethical transformation toward unbridled self-interest described first by Max Weber in his classic, *The Protestant Ethic and the Spirit of Capitalism*, took hold—economics in the "west" was the moral relations of individuals in the household, and the public household operated upon similar moral principles and relations, or at least pretended to, under the name moral philosophy. Modern economics became a subject of scientific and statistical inquiry when it separated from both the actual household and from abstract moral philosophy. And prior to Aristotle's discussion was what Mircea Eliade calls "the economy of the sacred," [4] the human communal connection with divinity. For archaic man the natural and human worlds were not separate from the sacred, transcendent world. The first was its physical embodiment, the second its cultural manifestation, the arena where natural ecology was turned into human economy.

The early economy of the sacred was the rites associated with women and fertility and men and virility, with sky gods and earth goddesses uniting. Later notions were cast in the language of the effulgence of life, of divine overflow, of the gifts of God, the abundance of the divine storehouse, with bounty and fecundity: indeed, with images and metaphors of wealth and well-being of all kinds. The whole multi-millennial movement from Earth Mother to Heavenly Father, and then from divine Personality to abstract Principle, shows, even now, the vestiges of this human relation with the Divine, the relation being the receiving of abundance when living in accordance with our proper nature.

Put in modern conceptual terms, these earlier formulations saw the material economy, so vaunted in the modern world, as comprising the set of material relations embedded within and reflecting a larger system of human moral relations which were, in turn, expressions of a complex social relation with the sacred: this last kept everything grounded in a higher moral and communal purpose. We have lost any real sense of the sacred and in so doing have lost belief in ourselves, leaving only things and our relations with them.

In this essay I mean economics in its Aristotelian sense of "household" relations between family members. But I mean these relations, which I name the moral economy, to refer to exchanges of values that spiritually bind together the members of the family of man: the household of humanity. These are the actions that you and I can do for each other when we meet on the street or at work, or get together in our homes, parks, malls, and neighborhoods. As the material economy generates more material wealth, so the moral economy increases society's moral wealth, which I call riches.

The moral economy appears and comes into view at this interpersonal level that operates in-between the individual and the institutional. As I see it, it works through three core principles: sharing, service, and self-sacrifice. That is, individuals sharing their material wealth, serving others, and sacrificing their personal interests for a common or collective good. Now, all economies have a moral dimension to them. But the moral economy of any materialist society is built on values opposed to the moral economy of this essay. The moral economy of materialism, especially its modern consumerist form, is composed of values and principles that promote actions and attitudes that are selfish, self-serving and self-centered. This is supposed to generate wealth, security and well-being, and for a time it does, but over time it does just the opposite. If one wants wealth, security, and well-being one must follow the principle of Jesus: "For whosoever will save his life shall lose it: and whosoever will lose his life for my sake shall find it." [5]

To build a real moral economy means, then, to return to our sacred origins, not historically but essentially, not to the past but to the roots of our being, for the moral economy is part of a larger economy, the Divine Economy, "that social code", [6] which is human collective relations mediated and enhanced through institutions and laws that regulate the global household on divine principles, a relationship captured in the Christian prayer, "on earth as it is in heaven". Exploring the nature and structure of that Divine Economy is another work. [7] (A concise but comprehensive outline of the workings of such a system was given by 'Abdu'l-Baha early last century. It can be found as Appendix One at the end of the essay.)

In a rapidly globalizing world, a true moral economy can only be founded upon the principle and ideal of the oneness of humanity, and the moral virtues of economic life must express, support and reinforce that ideal. [8] The oneness of humanity appears and operates within economic life when sharing spirit, not material gain, is the goal of human exchange, though, again, a proper material gain for everyone involved is needed. The moral economy works best when we spend material wealth for the common good, along with our inner spiritual riches, such as love, trust, and justice, which are as the different denominations of a spiritual currency. What are primarily exchanged through currency and labor in the material economy are goods and services. What is primarily exchanged through values in the moral economy is our noble humanity. In the first each values his personal profit, in the second each values the other.

Being victims of an improper education we must ask: What is a proper one? It cannot be simply a matter of wringing new information from an old and dry paradigm of understanding of human nature and the world. One comprehensive model of a proper education is found in my book, *Renewing the Sacred*, [9] and the statements on education woven throughout this essay are in a very real sense supplemental to *Renewing the Sacred*. This education is, at this point, idealistic of course, but short-sighted pragmatism, whether as educational philosophy or philosophy of action and purpose, has failed to inspire and give any clear direction. It merely careens from one crisis to the next with no vision of how to develop human society let alone stabilize itself.

There is another kind of practicality. 'Abdu'l-Baha was once rightly praised for walking the mystical path with practical feet. For the practical-minded, the following pages may seem an example of walking the practical path with mystical feet. But this higher path of practicality is not a Neverland of impossibly rosy wishes and Peter Pan happy thoughts. Just because something is not practiced does not necessarily mean it is not practical. Regarding the other practicality, the Universal House of Justice wrote: "There are spiritual principles, or what some call human values, by which solutions can be found for every social problem. Any well-intentioned group can in a general sense devise practical solutions to its problems, but good intentions and practical knowledge are usually not enough. The essential merit of spiritual principle is that it not only presents a perspective which harmonizes with that which is immanent in human nature, it also induces an attitude, a dynamic, a will, an aspiration, which facilitate the discovery and implementation of practical measures. Leaders of governments and all in authority would be well served in their efforts to solve problems if they would first seek to identify the principles involved and then be guided by them." [10]

A Look Inside

The first chapter follows the advice of the House of Justice and seeks to identify the fundamental spiritual principles involved in establishing a context for creating prosperity. It is titled, Wisdom and Wealth: The Catalyst of Transformation, because both spiritual wisdom **and** material wealth are needed for humanity to achieve prosperity. The prerequisite for that achievement, however, is what the House of Justice calls a spiritual revival that works to transform individuals who, in turn, can become the catalyst for changes in the social, political and economic spheres of collective life. This is social change through spiritual transformation. To see what would constitute such a spiritual revival the chapter explores a quotation from the Universal House of Justice found in a letter dated November 19, 1974. There the House of Justice states that people desperately need to know how to live their lives. Knowing how to do this is actually a product of answering four questions, which the reader will find stated there. Each chapter thereafter answers one of the four central questions. This book ends with a statement called Final Thoughts. (Note: As this book was going to print another book, *With Thine Own Eyes*, (George Ronald Press) came to my attention. Authors, Tomanio, Iverson, and Ring, explore with subtlety and insight the implications of these same questions within a context of investigating spiritual reality. Though written independently, the two books can easily be viewed as complementary studies.)

Finally, I should point out that, while the following discussion is supported almost entirely by statements from the Bahá'í Writings, this does not mean that I am presenting the "Bahá'í" solution to the economic problem. I am not. No official Bahá'í solution to the economic problem exists as yet, beyond certain general statements on ways to bring the material and spiritual dimensions of life into coherence. An example of such statements is, again, Appendix Two. This essay is but one Baha'i's attempt to address the economic problem, an attempt that grew from study of the Bahá'í Writings, yes, but it is not "the" Bahá'í perspective, rather, from first to last it is my own.

I chose this approach because the Bahá'í Writings are the ones I am most familiar with in this field of study. Other works, such as Martin Nowak's *Super Cooperators*[11] or Robert Axelrod's *Evolution of Cooperation*,[12] work similar ground from a scientific perspective. Too, there is a whole stream of books and articles appearing that explore topics like the relation between happiness and increased productivity, altruism as a drive shaping economic behavior, and the inverse correlation between class and ethical behavior.

Noteworthy here is the work of Paul Piff and his co-researchers in the study, *Higher Social Class Predicts Increased Unethical Behavior.* [13] Piff et al. demonstrated a direct and inverse correlation between wealth and increasingly unethical behavior, with behaviors such as selfishness, lying and cheating, more prevalent among the most well-to-do. They found that the unethical behavior of the rich stems from a strong sense of personal entitlement, which, in turn, is rationalized by self-deceiving validations of their right to possess great wealth fortified by moral justifications for selfishness. All seems, finally, to be grounded in their more favorable attitudes toward greed, as was brilliantly dramatized, for example, in the movie *Wall Street.*

As one moves up the ladder of "success", the ideology of self-interest becomes more attractive, and dreams of personal accomplishment are increasingly pursued to the detriment of others and to one's own higher impulses. Unsurprisingly, then, among the advantaged classes there is a corresponding falling off of feelings of compassion, of community, and of cooperation. This leads to a cascade of pernicious effects, all ending in the unprecedented levels of economic inequality now present in American society and elsewhere. But the studies also show that higher impulses can often be reawakened and measureable levels of change in values can be detected when the rich are exposed to scenes that evoke compassion and sympathy. That is, through appeals to higher human nature, the destructive ideology of selfish competition can be changed into a constructive life of selfless cooperation.

This is fascinating and timely scholarship and such works need to be read to round out the whole picture and to put the argument of this essay on a more scientific footing. But scripture has its place, both as generator of knowledge and motivator of moral behavior, so that any discussion wishing to advance the field of economics can take account of both science and religion, for each sheds valuable light upon the other and on the whole field.

Wisdom and Wealth:
The Catalyst of Transformation

Why—and the question needs to be asked plainly—has this society been impotent, despite its great wealth, to remove the injustices that are tearing its fiber apart? The answer to this question, as amply evidenced by decades of contentious history, cannot be found in political passion, conflicting expressions of class interest, or technical recipes. What is called for is a spiritual revival, as a prerequisite to the successful application of political, economic and technological instruments. But there is a need for a catalyst.
(The Universal House of Justice, 2000 Jan 08)

     Truth is a condition of unity. Unity is not two things as the same thing, but two conditions, outer and inner, in resonant harmony manifesting one thing in their coherent interaction.

     My thesis is that general prosperity endures only when our outer material and inner spiritual aspects are operating in balance. Although the terms riches and wealth can obviously be used interchangeably, in this essay I will use the term riches to refer to the spiritual form of wealth, and the word wealth to mean the material form of riches. Riches, which are moral virtues, and wealth, broadly speaking, our material goods, are, from this perspective, complementary aspects of true prosperity; one without the other is insufficient and leads to poverty. The world today overemphasizes the material side and that is why we are experiencing economic meltdown. Hence, we must re-establish a balance between spiritual riches and material wealth. How to do this? That deceptively simple question requires too complex an answer for this essay or my knowledge. Rather, I will ask: What can education do to help achieve balance?

We can start by making a simple, perhaps overly-simple, distinction about economic problems, namely, that there are two main types of them: too little and too much. These are never far apart. In our economically integrated world, the problem of too little for many occurs because a few have too much. That is as true for individuals as it is for nations. [1] A material underdevelopment among many occurs because of the spiritual underdevelopment of some few. That, I feel, is the essence, of a complex and intricate problem whose solution must also include the changing of social and economic institutions at every level.

To solve the problem of too little requires, first, setting in place a practical and intellectual education that enables disadvantaged people to acquire the skills needed to obtain what they materially need. But this addresses only one half of the problem, and by itself spawns a wriggling mass of other challenges, for it only better enables some previously unfortunate individuals to insert themselves somewhere into an increasingly dysfunctioning system. In short, this "fix" creates even more competition for a shrinking economic pie, generating ever more frustration, resentment, rage and anxiety. This toxic mix will explode. There is little doubt of that. A solution that "fixes" only half a problem is no real solution at all, but adds to the severity and urgency of the problem.

To address the second problem, of a few holding too much, requires a moral and spiritual education which persuades the well-to-do that doing everything possible to empower those less fortunate is in everybody's best interest. In either case, proper education is a key element of a spiritual solution to economic problems. But since the problem of too little is really a result of some having too much and not sharing, then the real problem for education must be a rethinking of the main purpose of education itself, away from academic and technical training for mere personal advantage to moral and spiritual enlightenment for the advantage of all. Fixing material poverty is, from this view, a product of fixing spiritual poverty, for, in truth, there is plenty of wealth to go around. It is spiritual riches that are scarce and remain undeveloped. A new impetus for change is required.

That is a challenge for proper education to meet. As this essay is not really about the practical training of people for employment, i.e. equipping them with the skills of providing material necessities for family and community, and the like, the primary discussion here is on the spiritual side, namely, the educing and training of individual moral capacity to create the context for universal prosperity within spiritualized community.

The Universal House of Justice stated what I believe are the four pillars of this perspective for spiritual education: "It is not merely material well-being that people need. What they desperately need is to know how to live their lives—they need to know who they are, to what purpose they exist, and how they should act towards one another; and, once they know the answers to these questions they need to be helped to gradually apply these answers to everyday behaviour. It is to the solution of this basic problem of mankind that the greater part of all our energy and resources should be directed." (2)

For the Good of our Fellow Man

The first thing that strikes us about this concise statement from the Universal House of Justice is that the situation, even in 1974 when the paragraph was composed, was "desperate." Though unprecedented numbers of people were "well off" materially, they needed to know how to live with this affluence. Self-knowledge, not money, was in desperately short supply. This was "the basic problem of mankind."

Indeed, as the Bahá'í Revelation appeared more than one hundred fifty years ago, and given that this principle was part of Bahá'í teachings from its beginning, the "problem" is at least that old. In the mid-nineteenth century, Bahá'u'lláh perceived the signs of disaster gathering on the near horizon of the future. He wrote: "The winds of despair are, alas, blowing from every direction, and the strife that divideth and afflicteth the human race is daily increasing. The signs of impending convulsions and chaos can now be discerned, inasmuch as the prevailing order appeareth to be lamentably defective."[3] One hundred years later, in 1974, to call the situation "desperate" is not shrill overstatement, but almost subdued understatement. Today, another forty years later, even the most jaded observer sees it.

The only meaningful first implication one can draw from the phrase "need to know how to live their lives" is that many people don't know how to live their lives—though they probably think that they do, or don't know any better than what they are currently doing. The paragraph then goes on to pose some very ideal criteria for knowing how to live one's life, criteria seemingly far removed from the ordinary activities we normally associate with that phrase. But if, as the House of Justice says elsewhere: "The primary task of the soul will always be to investigate reality, to live in accordance with the truths of which it becomes persuaded and to accord full respect to the efforts of others to do the same", [4] then these criteria follow quite naturally, for they are all developed by proper education and seem to have some close relation with achieving prosperity.

Is there a secret that unlocks this hidden knowledge? Well, yes and no. In truth, the essence of it is found in all religious scripture and is known as the Golden Rule, so it is no secret. But we do seem to need to have it repeated again and again. One Bahá'í version of it is this: "We must be like the fountain or spring that is continually emptying itself of all that it has, and is continually being refilled from an invisible source. To be continually giving out for the good of our fellows undeterred by the fear of poverty and reliant on the unfailing bounty of the Source of all wealth and all good—that is the secret of right living." [5]

There is a great deal to ponder in this short statement. First, the secret of right living does not exclude generating wealth. Wealth is not frowned upon in the Bahá'í Teachings. As in all religions, however, material wealth is regarded as potentially a real barrier to personal and collective spiritual growth and development, a barrier which if overcome brings great rewards and powers. "Know ye in truth", Bahá'u'lláh writes, "that wealth is a mighty barrier between ... the lover and his beloved... Well is it then with him who, being rich, is not hindered by his riches from the eternal Kingdom... The splendor of such a wealthy man shall illuminate the dwellers of heaven even as the sun enlightens the earth!" (6)

'Abdu'l-Bahá wrote: "Wealth is praiseworthy in the highest degree, if it is acquired by an individual's own effort and the grace of God, in commerce, agriculture, art and industry, and if it be expended for philanthropic purposes…Wealth is most commendable, provided the entire population is wealthy." (7) So, just working hard and ethically to get personal wealth does not earn much applause. Prosperity enjoins the creation of wealth if that wealth enriches all, is acquired properly, and is spent for the common good. The real wealth in wealth, then, is what one expends for the good of others. The Bahá'í Writings never define prosperity as just having general material plenty, as that is measured by some wholly numerical and abstract economic indictors, such as Gross National Product, nor deems prosperity as some having more than they can consume when others have less than they need. For me, prosperity is when every single person has enough and not a person before. But we will never achieve that goal without a sympathetic heart and mind, and an organic change in the structure of society that embodies spiritual principles of love and justice.

Neither does the secret of right living discount trusting the "invisible" to refill our personal and collective accounts. In fact, it relies on this recompense, knowing that with God "is the storehouse of all that is in heaven and earth." (8) If, as 'Abdu'l-

Baha said, "the fundamentals of the whole economic condition are divine in nature and are associated with the world of the heart and spirit," then economic challenges are never adequately met through purely material or only human efforts. God intends humanity to be prosperous. Indeed, our Creator is indispensable to this. But His wish can best be realized only if enough people are willing to be like that fountain that empties itself of all that it has for the good of others. If we refuse to let Him be involved, He does not turn away, but finds ways to bring us back into proper relation with Him, with each other, and with the earth. We call these interpositions recessions, depressions and cataclysms that result from not acting in conformity with universal moral principles, such as love thy neighbor, which are found in every spiritual tradition.

Lastly, we should give, "undeterred by the fear of poverty" and be reliant on the "unfailing bounty of the Source of all wealth." But we should not paint too rosy a picture. Giving will generate the fear of loss. It is human nature, at least our lower nature, to fear that in giving to others one is impoverishing oneself. Fear will be there! But we must not be deterred by it. It helps to overcome this natural fear by believing that the "bounty of the Source of all wealth" is "unfailing." That is, giving actually enriches not impoverishes the giver. In words echoed in all spiritual traditions, 'Abdu'l-Baha said: "Eternal happiness is contingent upon giving." [9] In the same light, the Buddha is reported to have remarked: "If you knew what I know about the power of giving, you would not let a single meal pass without sharing it in some way."

It is not that we must either be happy "here" on earth or happy "there" in heaven, because, spiritually, here is the anteroom of there. The goal is for everyone to be happy all the time. Giving does not mean throwing wealth away mindlessly and indiscriminately in some moral spasm of guilt or mawkish sentimentality, but to use personal wealth to create wealth for all: that is, use wealth to create more riches because more riches creates more wealth. This is the sociological version of the old adage: "Give a man a fish and feed him for a day. Teach a man to fish and you feed him for the rest of his life." But it has this further twist: if you also ask him to share his new fishing knowledge, then others can be fed for the rest of their lives.

Also, "to be reliant on the unfailing bounty of the Source of all wealth" does not mean to ask and then sit idly for manna to fall from heaven. It means effort and striving so that the moving ship can be steered towards its proper port.

In the two sentences of Shoghi Effendi's statement, then, are found the main connections and interactions between the spiritual and material aspects of prosperity. But the spiritual must be primary. As Shoghi Effendi said: "Laws and institutions, as viewed by Bahá'u'lláh, can become really effective only when our inner spiritual life has been perfected and transformed." (9)

Within the perspective set by this statement on the secret of right living we can explore in some depth the above statement of the House of Justice, for it is the key to knowing how to achieve prosperity. But some pretty formidable spiritual and social barriers to knowing and doing have been erected. These will have to be identified so they may be demolished. That will take place later. But all barriers are connected with the phrase "lack of a proper education." Tearing down these barriers is the result of the application of our critical intelligence. Building something new in their stead grows from another power, envisioning. So we must ask: What are the parameters of a proper education as we will use the term?

A Proper Education

A proper education means more than learning a body of academic knowledge, or a set of skills related to gaining employment, or passively conforming to a cultural canon of beliefs and assumptions about Reality. 'Abdu'l-Baha explains that "education is of various kinds. There is a training and development of the physical body which ensures strength and growth. There is intellectual education or mental training for which schools and colleges are founded. The third kind of education is that of the spirit. Through the breaths of the Holy Spirit man is uplifted into the world of moralities and illumined by the lights of divine bestowals. The moral world is only attained through the effulgence of the Sun of Reality and the quickening life of the divine spirit. For this reason the holy Manifestations of God appear in the human world." **(10)**

In another place the Bahá'í Faith teaches: "In the Bahá'í view, the education required to enrich the human mind and spirit must seek to develop those essentially moral attributes—including truthfulness, courtesy, generosity, compassion, justice, love, and trustworthiness—whose reflection in the everyday lives of human beings can create harmonious, productive families and communities and make the enjoyment of fundamental rights a reality for all their members. Such education, moreover, must help to instill in every individual a keen, emotionally grounded awareness of the fundamental unity of humankind. As people begin to see each other as members of one human family, they will become willing to discard negative learned stereotypes and begin to see people of other ethnic groups, nationalities, classes and religious beliefs as potential friends rather than as threats or enemies." **(11)**

A proper education conforms with and provides forms for the expression of essential human nature. (We'll look at that nature in more detail in the next section.) The basic content of such a proper education is called "spiritual principles." These are statements such as, "Love thy neighbor as thyself", and the purpose of such statements is to train people to appropriate moral action. They work because spiritual principles educe, or bring forth, moral potentialities, called human values, such as, love, justice, and trustworthiness, which are innate attributes of the essential human reality, and give them manifest form, called virtues. Being human values they are honored in every culture.

A similar relationship works in other aspects of learning. Mathematics, for example, trains certain intellectual potentialities for understanding the logic of numbers and manipulating quantities and the relations of quantities. Learning language does the same for our verbal potentialities, making them into the abilities of reading, writing and speaking.

Articulated spiritual principles resonate with the inner potentialities of the human reality to make a harmonic unity, like the blending of the bass and treble of the musical scale, which is the condition of truth. Unity is manifest at the level of coordination of interests. Spiritual principles not only educe the innate spiritual attributes of the human essence, but also over time expand their range and power. Spiritual principles recur with every revelation from God, for continuing to send Revelation is God's moral relation with humankind. Revelation, according to Bahá'í belief, is progressive. Hence these principles are given new application and wider expression when they are restated in new form within a new revelation. A proper education also includes the bringing forth of these virtues in a form appropriate to the needs of the age in order to transform the human world.

For example, all religions stress the virtue of loving one's neighbor. In past ages, one's neighbors were the members of one's clan, or tribe, or city, or nation. But, in a globalizing world, the idea of neighbor must expand to include every human being on the planet. Hence Baha'u'llah says: "The highest essence and most perfect expression of whatsoever the peoples of old have either said or written hath, through this most potent Revelation, been sent down from the heaven of the Will of the All-Possessing, the Ever-Abiding God. Of old it hath been revealed: 'Love of one's country is an element of the Faith of God.' The Tongue of Grandeur hath, however, in the day of His manifestation proclaimed: 'It is not his to boast who loveth his country, but it is his who loveth the world." [12]

Inculcating spiritual principles in human consciousness so they can guide human action is the foundation and goal of a proper education. But a proper education also includes physical and mental training. These must include the ways to acquire knowledge, cultivate the powers of intellect and reasoning, teach practical skills for earning one's livelihood, nurture the desire for excellence, and inculcate a dedication to service. This last is most important, for action in service, which is virtue, completes the connection between inner spirit and outer world and enables the transformative current of energy to flow.

This comprehensive approach to education should not go on only within our formal institutions of learning, but also be part of everyone's daily social and personal interaction. It must be embodied in the workings of social institutions, pervade the media, be part of civic discussion, and preached from pulpits. Every human interaction can be a laboratory where the efficacy of the hypothesis that the solution to our economic problem, indeed almost any problem, comes from identifying and applying spiritual principle, can be tested, refined and tried again. There is nothing really new in the theory and program I just outlined. It is just that we have not really tried it, or tried it for very long and in sufficient numbers. What is new today is that we have no other choice. We can wait no longer. The sphere of action is global, and the challenge is the same at every level: to grow spiritually.

The first part of knowing how to live life is to know who you are. So, let us go to the first question and ask:

Who Are You?

"...man should know his own self and recognize that which leadeth unto loftiness or lowliness, glory or abasement, wealth or poverty.
(Bahá'u'lláh, *Tablets of Bahá'u'lláh*: 34)

Every individual is a combination of racial background and cultural heritage, of family tradition and genetic DNA, of personal experience and playful imagination. All these have a part in forming each person, of course, but none of these is the essence of a human being. They are inherited or acquired characteristics and qualities, outer forms and patterns through which an inner essence finds expression. Thus the question, Who are you? is really after something more fundamental. What is really being asked is: Who are you as a spiritual being?
'Abdu'l-Baha explains that every individual possesses three characters: the innate character, the inherited character, and the acquired character gained by education.
"With regard to the innate character, although the divine creation is purely good, yet the varieties of natural qualities in man come from the difference of degree; all are excellent, but they are more or less so, according to the degree. So all mankind possess intelligence and capacities, but the intelligence, the capacity and the worthiness of men differ. This is evident."
The second character He calls the inherited character. "The variety of inherited qualities comes from strength and weakness of constitution—that is to say, when the two parents

are weak, the children will be weak; if they are strong, the children will be robust. In the same way, purity of blood has a great effect; for the pure germ is like the superior stock which exists in plants and animals. For example, you see that children born from a weak and feeble father and mother will naturally have a feeble constitution and weak nerves; they will be afflicted and will have neither patience, nor endurance, nor resolution, nor perseverance, and will be hasty; for the children inherit the weakness and debility of their parents....Hence it is evident that inherited character also exists..."

There is, finally, the third or acquired character gained from education. "But the difference of the qualities with regard to culture is very great, for education has great influence. Through education the ignorant become learned; the cowardly become valiant. Through cultivation the crooked branch becomes straight; the acid, bitter fruit of the mountains and woods becomes sweet and delicious; and the five-petaled flower becomes hundred petaled. Through education savage nations become civilized, and even the animals become domesticated. Education must be considered as most important, for as diseases in the world of bodies are extremely contagious, so, in the same way, qualities of spirit and heart are extremely contagious. Education has a universal influence, and the differences caused by it are very great." [1]

The word "character" comes from metallurgy and the casting of coins, the character being the imprint laid upon the molten blob of metal. For this essay, the innate character, the Divine imprint which is our unique soul, is all those God-given abilities, qualities, and capacities we carry into the world. It is what we "inherently possess." The inherited character, the genetic inheritance of physical and mental qualities that is the biological imprint from blood parents and ancestors, further defines our individuality. Spiritual and biological potentialities are actualized and trained—enhanced, changed, modified, or restricted—by the acquired character, the social imprint of learned abilities and skills acquired from social life, especially from education—a word meaning "to bring forth." To extend the metaphor in economic language, we can say that we possess or have access to spiritual capital, natural capital, and social capital. Where and how we invest our capital shows what we value in life and gives us return on living. Helping people decide the best way to invest their capital and giving them the instruments, skills and knowledge to grow that investment, is one purpose of education, our social capital. So the first thing that education does is to bring forth the individual by inculcating the skills and attitudes and developing the abilities to manifest his powers and talents or overcome his weaknesses.

"Education," the Master wrote, "cannot alter the inner essence of a man, but it doth exert tremendous influence, and with this power it can bring forth from the individual whatever perfections and capacities are deposited within him....Thus it is clearly demonstrated that by their essential nature, minds vary as to their capacity, while education also playeth a great role and exerteth a powerful effect on their development." (2)

Three Kinds of Education

We have three characters and, perhaps for symmetry, 'Abdu'l-Bahá also explained that: "Education is of three kinds: material, human and spiritual. Material education is concerned with the progress and development of the body, through gaining its sustenance, its material comfort and ease. This education is common to animals and man.

Human education signifies civilization and progress—that is to say, government, administration, charitable works, trades, arts and handicrafts, sciences, great inventions and discoveries and elaborate institutions, which are the activities essential to man as distinguished from the animal.

Divine education is that of the Kingdom of God: it consists in acquiring divine perfections, and this is true education; for in this state man becomes the focus of divine blessings, the manifestation of the words, "Let Us make man in

Our image, and after Our likeness." This is the goal of the world of humanity." (3)

In another place, He reiterated this view: "But education is of various kinds. There is a training and development of the physical body which ensures strength and growth. There is intellectual education or mental training for which schools and colleges are founded. The third kind of education is that of the spirit. Through the breaths of the Holy Spirit man is uplifted into the world of moralities and illumined by the lights of divine bestowals. The moral world is only attained through the effulgence of the Sun of Reality and the quickening life of the divine spirit. For this reason the holy Manifestations of God appear in the human world." (4)

Education is how the potentialities and powers latent within the human reality, whether physical, mental or spiritual, are brought forth, or left undeveloped. If the three kinds of education bring forth the whole character of human beings, why is human development not a simple and straightforward process? The reason it is not simple and straightforward lies in our nature, for when we look at human nature we see that it is actually two natures composed of seemingly opposing qualities. Education has a different role to play here. It must navigate a labyrinth of competing moral impulses. Morally, education directs the soul either toward the natural or toward the spiritual, either harmonizes the powers and potentialities of these natures or turns them against each other. The real question is: What character will be acquired from education?

Light and Dark: Joining the Moral Opposites

'Abdu'l-Baha wrote: "In man there are two natures; his spiritual or higher nature and his material or lower nature. In one he approaches God, in the other he lives for the world alone. Signs of both these natures are to be found in men. In his material aspect he expresses untruth, cruelty and injustice; all these are the outcome of his lower nature. The attributes of his Divine nature are shown forth in love, mercy, kindness, truth and justice, one and all being expressions of his higher nature. Every good habit, every noble quality belongs to man's spiritual nature, whereas all his imperfections and sinful actions are born of his material nature." (5)

In one place He called the higher nature man's "essential perfection" and his lower nature "absolute imperfection". (6) He also said: "For the inner reality of man is a demarcation line between the shadow and the light, a place where the two seas meet; it is the lowest point on the arc of descent, and therefore is it capable of gaining all the grades above. With education it can achieve all excellence; devoid of education it will stay on, at the lowest point of imperfection.

Every child is potentially the light of the world—and at the same time its darkness; wherefore must the question of education be accounted as of primary importance." (7)

The controlling metaphor here is light and darkness. In the contrast of essential perfection and absolute imperfection a polarity of opposites is set up which is the structure of human nature in this world. Because of this inherent opposition, 'Abdu'l-Baha stated: "Not in any other of the species in the world of existence is there such a difference, contrast, contradiction and opposition as in the species of man." (8)

A structure of opposites is always needed for a flow of energy to happen, so that training, progress and the manifesting of potentialities into actualities may occur, "development" meaning making the human being more perfect in some way. That is hard work. Proper education is the means to overcome the inherent contradiction that is the moral opposition within human nature. Improper education is the path to destruction.

Shoghi Effendi further clarifies the nature of the soul, writing: "First concerning the human soul and its nature. According to the Bahá'í conception, the soul of man, or in other words his inner spiritual self or reality, is not dualistic. There is no such thing, as the Zoroastrians believe, as a double reality in man, a definite higher self and lower self. The latter is capable of development in either way. All depends fundamentally on the training or education which man receives. Human nature is made up of possibilities for both good and evil. True religion can enable it to soar in the highest realm of the spirit, while its absence can, as we already witness around us, cause it to fall to the lowest depth of degradation and misery." [9]

Thus the two natures are, from this perspective, the beginning and end states of the soul. How does the soul go from one state to another? Somewhat like a lamp on a rheostat, a dimmer switch, the soul can progress from dark and unlit to full brightness. Keeping the image of two states *and* the progress of the soul in mind, we can say that there is the initial state, which has all the grades of spirit within it as potential, and the intended spiritual state, which is the transformed spiritually mature soul. The first state is what every soul is at birth. While this state is "purely good", it is also only more or less so and is called dark. That is, it is good, but imperfect. The second state is what every soul can become when it is enkindled. What the soul becomes, Shoghi Effendi pointed out, "depends fundamentally on the training or education which man receives": or, as the Master warned: "With education it can achieve all excellence; devoid of education it will stay on, at the lowest point of imperfection."

Similarly, in relation to development, consider the human body. At conception it is but a single fertilized cell, yet that cell holds the entire body within it as potential. At maturity, the intended state, the body is fully grown, and all the physical powers and capacities latent within that single cell are manifest, provided the individual has received proper nourishment and exercise. The flower, too, begins as a seed, which under proper care develops roots, stem, leaves and results in a beautiful, fragrant blossom. In like manner, the first state of the soul is as the seed of spiritual potential. But in its intended state, a state which can only be reached through the fertilizing and nurturing power of divine education, it appears in the full stature and glory of spirituality. In all cases, whether that of the flower, the body, or the soul, the wise and patient teacher will see the end in the beginning and looking to the intended, fully realized state, train the body, the flower, or the soul, to reach its condition of utmost beauty and glory. Yet in whatever state it may be, the soul is always and only one reality.

Underdevelopment

The name often used to refer to the darker nature is "ego". But this is not exactly true for us. Ego is, for me, not the name for some separate dark nature, as, in a similarly mistaken fashion, Satan is the name given to some independent evil power in the moral universe. Rather, ego is the undeveloped soul, the soul lead astray by following improper gods. Remember, the soul is ever one reality, with possibilities for both good and evil within it. Its first state, though imperfect, is not evil, but purely good. The ego is that center of self around which cluster those possibilities for evil that have remained in an untransformed state. They are the natural inclinations for narrow self-interest that have not been turned into spiritual impulses for selflessness. The ego is the hard seed that needs to break open so that the virtues latent within it may flower.

As the name for this state of moral underdevelopment, the ego is a psychological construct composed of all those deeply held beliefs that convince us of our separateness from God and each other. These often subconscious beliefs are held together through the dynamics of guilt, fear, repression and projection, creating the appearance that the ego is a separate entity by keeping the person spiritually cut off and unconscious of higher realities. These ego-built opaque veils separate and isolate the individual, and he can get so walled up within himself that the divine light cannot penetrate. The ego's forms are legion, its powers are finite, but its appetites are infinite. It is "multiple identities that were born of passion and desire." [10] It is divisive, separating, competitive, and atomistic, because it is spiritually immature.

The ego always sees itself as the good side of an oppositional polarity, or as the victim of some evil toward itself.

To it whatever is opposite or outside it is the enemy and is to be destroyed or propitiated. The ego's moral world is built upon me first. Because of this distortion in thinking the ego-dominated person flees from his own best interests, which are identical to those of the common good, and clings to material self-interest, which is not. It is about unchaining such a self that Baha'u'llah wrote: "And amongst the realms of unity is the unity of rank and station...Ever since the seeking of preference and distinction came into play, the world hath been laid waste. It hath become desolate." [11]

The spiritual nature is the divine image imprinted upon the human reality when it comes under the influence of divine education. It is one identity of many attributes and qualities. The spiritual nature is a complex unity, embracing, purposeful, integrated, and cooperative. The material nature is a complex jumble of parts not in harmony even with each other, for its fractious passions are at war jockeying to be top dog. If the material nature is passionate, the spiritual nature is compassionate. At the ego level we are conflict-driven creatures, continually striving to overcome others and the limitations that are perceived as oppositions imposed by outer and inner constraints. No matter how much one's "education" may say so, the ego is not our real nature, but is like a bad passport photo of our true self, which is the higher self.

Every soul represents the spiritual capital of the whole human race, but each soul is a unique individual configuration of that capital. Every individual has all human qualities, both positive and negative, because every human being is all the qualities of God, and each quality of light casts a shadow, which is the lower self. Abdu'l-Baha states: "...knowledge is a quality of man, and so is ignorance; truthfulness is a quality of man; so is falsehood; trustworthiness and treachery, justice and injustice, are qualities of man, and so forth. Briefly, all the perfections and virtues, and all the vices, are qualities of man." [12]

We see that, no matter what the image employed, at the level of structure, the natures and their qualities seem to be locked into a competitive zero-sum game—i.e. the brighter the light the deeper the shadow. Whatever truth there is to this view, it is not quite true. An increase of knowledge is certainly a decrease in ignorance, for ignorance is the want of knowledge. But knowledge is not the want of ignorance, except in some smoke and mirrors sophistry. Yet, on "The more you know the more you know that you don't know" principle, there is a sense in which qualities opposed in structure modulate into a developmental sequence. I mean that if knowledge is the end and opposite of ignorance, then ignorance can be the beginning and opposite of knowledge.

Seeing it this way shifts the discussion from the somewhat abstract, static pictures of character and nature used so far, to a grounded process of moral development of qualities from vice to virtue. That is, if vice is the want of some positive quality, as darkness is the absence of light, then a vice is really an empty form in need of content, like the vacuum state. The empty form of vice, then, is the first form of virtue, the need to fill it is the drive to acquire capacity. Capacity is developed when a quality transforms from one state to a higher one.

'Abdu'l-Baha explains: "In creation there is no evil; all is good. Certain qualities and natures innate in some men and apparently blameworthy are not so in reality. For example, from the beginning of his life you can see in a nursing child the signs of greed, of anger and of temper. Then, it may be said, good and evil are innate in the reality of man, and this is contrary to the pure goodness of nature and creation. The answer to this is that greed, which is to ask for something more, is a praiseworthy quality provided that it is used suitably. So if a man is greedy to acquire science and knowledge, or to become compassionate, generous and just, it is most praiseworthy. If he exercises his anger and wrath against the bloodthirsty tyrants who are like ferocious beasts, it is very praiseworthy; but if he does not use these qualities in a right way, they are blameworthy." [13]

Education, or bringing forth, is potential becoming actual, the switch from capacious to capacity that draws forth more potential. As darkness proves the existence of light, perhaps the way to view the lower nature of man is as the negative drive to advance spiritually. For example, though "material progress and spiritual progress are two very different things," [14] nonetheless, a century ago 'Abdu'l-Baha said of the Japanese: "Inasmuch as they have advanced in material civilization they must assuredly possess the capacity for spiritual development." [15] To bring forth the full positive potential of the human reality we should have appropriate models and metaphors for education to use. I mean we should not just thunder at the vices of humanity, such as greed, ignorance, and selfishness, and leave it at that. Rather, education must train the greedy one to pursue knowledge and be of service. But the only way to do this is through the third kind of education, divine education. Material and human education alone, or even together, will not accomplish this. Why?

Metaphors, Images, Symbols

Bahá'u'lláh calls the human reality "a mine rich in gems of inestimable value." He goes on to state how this ideal mine is connected with education: "Education can, alone, cause it to reveal its treasures and enable mankind to benefit therefrom." Just prior to this metaphor of the mine rich in gems He called the human being "the supreme talisman", but warned: "lack of a proper education hath deprived him of that which he doth inherently possess." [16] Any education is improper education if it deprives people of knowing about the spiritual dimension of the world and themselves, though it may adequately inform them about the physical and intellectual dimensions.

The metaphors of a "mine rich in gems" and the "supreme talisman" refer to the essential, inborn nature, that innate character which is the human essence. Hence, in a statement such as: "Behold Me standing within thee, mighty, powerful and self-subsisting," [17] it seems that Bahá'u'lláh means by "Me" the likeness or similitude of the divinity within our being, our talismanic essence that as the "crown of creation" has all creation spiritually within it and can resonate with and attract all creation to it. To my mind, the talisman that is the human essence is the same as the Biblical: "Let us make man in our image, after our likeness." [18]

Now, a talisman needs to be properly magnetized. It is not that the human talisman is not magnetized today. It is that in our materialistic civilization the soul is magnetized almost entirely by crude and coarse material energies and vibrations. To be spiritually magnetized the soul must enter the charged field of the Word of God "inasmuch as these holy verses are the most potent elixir, the greatest and mightiest talisman," [19] and in this way enter into relation with one of God's Messengers, for the Prophet of God "is in truth the Supreme Talisman and is endowed with supernatural powers." [20] Informing us of what we inherently possess and educing that God-given inheritance by demonstrating the value of spiritual and moral action has been the mission of every Prophet and Manifestation of God.

I have explained that the soul is endowed with various moral potentialities of which the individual may be unaware, but which can be made manifest by personal volition in response to wishes, tests, and circumstances, or under the tutelage of spiritual principles and moral models. Perhaps the best way to manifest a virtue is by following a model. For the followers of every religion their Founder, whether Abraham, Moses, Buddha, Jesus or Muhammad, is their supreme model of virtue, and the Teachings each leaves behind are the source of human moral and social development, the educing forms that draw forth human potential by providing resonant principles to respond to.

Let us take faith as an example of such an inherent power that can be brought out by a model. 'Abdu'l-Bahá says: "Man is endowed with ideal virtues, for example intellection, volition–among them faith, confession and acknowledgment of God..." [21] The faith that human beings express is a reflection or likeness of the faithfulness that God through His Messengers shows us. That is, we know and express faith because God is first faithful towards us. But we also know faith by perceiving how another is faithful to principle, to belief, to conviction.

The Prophet's life and teachings provide exemplars for human thought and action. But more than this: Their Words and deeds are creative. They educe states of being from us. The Bahá'í Faith teaches: "The Messengers of God are not merely teachers, although this is one of their primary functions. Rather, the spirit of their words, together with the example of their lives, has the capacity to tap the roots of human motivation and to induce fundamental and lasting change." [22]

All human qualities are reflections of the qualities of God that are manifested for us by humanity's great Spiritual Luminaries. The image of God which is our higher self is the God within us recognizing its true Reality in the more perfect likeness of itself demonstrated by the life and teachings of the Prophet, and responding to it. But such recognition only occurs on condition that the inner "faculty" for recognizing Him has been developed so that the truth may be "imprinted" upon our beings, so to speak. Obscuring this process of recognition upon which all spiritual growth depends is exactly what an "improper education" does. It does this by defining "God" as merely a psychological projection of our own best image, and thus thick clouds of spiritual uncertainty form that obscure the radiant Light of the divine Sun. Man becomes enclosed within himself, locked up within his own subjectivity.

Others, too, try to tell us what we are. But if they start from the ego side, the side of need and desire, they do so to our detriment. Many observers of human nature, seeing a newborn, would argue that human beings are inherently poor, weak and helpless and some forms of education, often religious-based, subtlety prey on that debilitating idea, keeping people in a state of near total psychological dependence on outer things, other people, and circumstances of crisis. Bahá'u'lláh counters this crushing bit of psychological nonsense about humanity's supposed weakness with: "Dost thou reckon thyself only a puny form when within thee the universe is folded?" [23] Knowing the universe is enfolded within every soul, the divinely Educator is bewildered when people think of themselves as empty and impoverished. Speaking as the Voice of God He asks: "I created thee rich, why dost thou bring thyself down to poverty? Noble I made thee, wherewith dost thou abase thyself?" (24)

Clearly, Bahá'u'lláh Himself never experienced an improper education, or He wouldn't ask the question. He knew the answer, of course, but He asked the question of us so we would ask it of ourselves. He never became enmeshed in the abusive, choking tangles of learned impotence many people experience. He never lost sight of the truth that He was created rich. What is the result of having a proper education? "O My Servant! Obey Me and I shall make thee like unto Myself. I say 'Be,' and it is, and thou shalt say 'Be,' and it shall be." (25)

Other theorists may argue that we do not bring ourselves down to poverty, rather outer circumstances, such as destitution, sickness, and war, bring us down. However outwardly poor one may be, they say, each of us is full of unlimited creative intellectual potential and imaginative capacity. What is necessary to fix this felt inner poverty and to release these potentialities is to improve the outer circumstances. The Bahá'í Writings agree with this opinion, but go farther.

Certainly to increase people's physical and mental well-being is a good and noble goal, and it is some of those same creative mental potentialities that Bahá'u'lláh means by our riches. But I also think that Bahá'u'lláh means something far beyond what is meant by these qualities of body and mind, so that even the best of current education can only provide, from this view, a poverty of self-understanding if it leaves out spiritual instruction. Much of current secular education does precisely this. Really fixing this poverty of self-knowledge is done through exposure to living spiritual principle. This can overcome a tremendous amount of outer poverty because it empowers people to arise and themselves improve their circumstances. Such spiritual "aid" radically reduces the risk of engaging in sweet seductions of paternalistic do-goodism that breed dependency and that so often characterize well-meaning but subtly enslaving programs of material aid.

Finally, some might say that humanity can, unaided, lift itself out of its well of despair. Human reason and invention are adequate to any challenge, they argue. The proper moral behaviors and virtues that will enable us to work together to fix our troubles are known. It is simply a matter of putting them into practice. However, 'Abdu'l-Baha issues this quiet warning: "These virtues do not appear from the reality of man except through the power of God and the divine teachings, for they need supernatural power for their manifestation. It may be that in the world of nature a trace of these perfections may appear, but they are unstable and ephemeral; they are like the rays of the sun upon the wall." [26]

This last quote enables us to more fully grasp both the need and the dynamics of divine education, for it sheds light upon other statements in the Bahá'í Writings which seem to contradict the images of the "mine rich in gems" and a "supreme talisman" with a universe folded within it. In this regard, Baha'u'llah also wrote: "Thou art He, O God, Who hath proclaimed Himself as the Lord of Wealth, and characterized all that serve Him as poor and needy,"[27] and: "All are but poor and needy."[28] Indeed in one of their daily Obligatory Prayers Baha'is exclaim: "I testify, at this moment, to my powerlessness and to Thy might, to my poverty and to Thy wealth." [29] How can one reconcile statements that paint the human reality as both incalculably rich and powerful and abjectly poor and needy? How can a mine rich in gems, a supreme talisman with the universe folded within it, be poor and in need of anything?

While we are going to also look at this question a little later in a discussion about acquiring virtues, for now we should remember that, according the 'Abdu'l-Baha, moral virtues are not within human power to consistently manifest. He stated: "The moral world is only attained through the effulgence of the Sun of Reality and the quickening life of the divine spirit. For this reason the holy Manifestations of God appear in the human world." ⁽³⁰⁾ Human moral advance, both individually and collectively, is intimately tied to our connection with message of the Manifestations of God. By Their influence the darkness of the human world is illumined, and the dark coal of the lower nature is turned into sparkling diamonds of the higher nature.

The soul is a spiritual reality with infinite potential. The innate character is wholly good, though only more or less so, for every individual is imperfect. To advance spiritually is to move through stages of moral growth under the beneficent and guiding influence of the Word of God. The soul is completely dependent upon that spiritual influence for its advance. So the answer to our question is, we are immensely rich, but we are rich in all save God, poor in nothing save God. To be deprived of what we inherently possess is the same as being kept poor and needy of God.

In Bahá'u'lláh's mind, then, there is clearly a difference between an education which "educes" latent spiritual gems and "enables mankind to benefit therefrom" and much of what passes for education today, which is, from a moral and spiritual perspective, really a "lack of a proper education" for it deprives us of what we inherently possess, namely, our spiritual endowments, whatever it bestows of physical and intellectual learning. Improper education does this by distorting true human nature, marginalizing the importance of moral training, obscuring the value of practicing virtue, and denying the existence of the supernatural Power of our moral development. In short, if education focuses primarily on training the body and mind and does not give due attention to bringing forth what each soul "inherently" possesses, then that education is improper, and whatever benefits it gives humanity will be short-term benefits. As one document put it: "a well schooled person lacking in morals will tend to be harmful to the community, whereas a person with little or no formal education but with a strong sense of morality will, by and large, prove to be beneficial to society (of course, better that the individual be both formally educated and morally trained)." ⁽³¹⁾

What are the results of being deprived of what we inherently possess? There are many. I will concentrate on the two I feel are the most important. The first negatively affects the relationship each individual has with himself or herself, while the second cramps human social relationships. These deprivations make character development a crooked rather than a straight path, and knowing about them help us understand how we got into our current mess.

Deprivations

Foremost among those powers and faculties of which an improper education deprives us is the faculty of recognizing the Word of God Itself. For many religionists the relationship with God is an inherent one, and without it the mind and heart can make no coherent sense of the universe and themselves. Yet for those under the sway of a more limited secular system of belief, that relation with God is problematic at best, non-existent at worst. This humanistic, intellectualistic education has brought many benefits to humanity, but it has cost its proponents something necessary to be fully human. Bahá'u'lláh wrote: "Gracious God! It was intended that at the time of the manifestation of the One true God the faculty of recognizing Him would have been developed and matured and would have reached its culmination. However, it is now clearly demonstrated that in the unbelievers this faculty hath remained undeveloped and hath, indeed, degenerated." [32] This faculty is what enables the human heart to recognize the Voice of God as uniquely different from any human voice. This is the faculty which perceives either the divine Message or the divinity within things. This faculty responds to the divine Message to uplift human moral capacity and virtue. It puts us in touch with God.

Lack of a proper education also deprives the individual from believing himself or herself to be a "supreme talisman" with terrific powers. A lack of understanding regarding our true nature has helped to bring about the economic crisis. The House of Justice wrote: "This unprecedented economic crisis, together with the social breakdown it has helped to engender, reflects a profound error of conception about human nature itself. For the levels of response elicited from human beings by the incentives of the prevailing order are not only inadequate, but seem almost irrelevant in the face of world events. We are being shown that, unless the development of society finds a purpose beyond the mere amelioration of material conditions, it will fail of attaining even these goals. That purpose must be sought in spiritual dimensions of life and motivation that transcend a constantly changing economic landscape and an artificially imposed division of human societies into "developed" and "developing". (33)

The social result of being deprived of what we inherently possess is that discord and malice, perversity and rancor, have come to characterize much of modern life. More than one hundred years ago Bahá'u'lláh lamented: "No two men can be found who may be said to be outwardly and inwardly united. The evidences of discord and malice are apparent everywhere, though all were made for harmony and union." (34) The situation has, on most fronts, only worsened, though encouraging signs of humanity's spiritualization and unification are there to see. But the deeper point here is that disharmony and disunity either within the human soul, or between people, is not a God-created condition, but a human-created one, since human beings were created for "harmony and union." It should, therefore, be easier to cooperate in unity than to compete in disunity, as it is easier to smile than to frown. But to live in unity, individuals must perceive and act from the higher nature.

Living without a proper understanding of human nature and within a condition of extreme disunity leads to an inchoate psychological counter-thrust where "more and more people from all strata of society frantically seek their true identity, which is to say, although they would not so plainly admit it, the spiritual meaning of their lives." (35)

Being "made for harmony and union" and "created to show forth love" is a statement about our essential nature. Said another way, cooperation, not competition, is and has always been the key to the evolution. Baha'u'llah's statement puts to rest all theories of human nature which say humans are only selfish, conflict-driven creatures. Rather, an improper education skews our vision toward the selfish side of our nature, depriving us of understanding this deep, innate nature of harmony and union. It hides this deeper nature from view, because it confines itself to material self-interest, and so prevents us from acting on that understanding; namely that spiritual self-interest is actually self-sacrifice. Yet, in truth it is a self-fulfilling prophecy. Being deprived of knowledge of our true selves, we do, indeed, become conflict-driven, because false identity is the same as our own destruction.

While it may be hard to believe that, given humanity's bloodstained past, unity, reciprocity and cooperation are possible to achieve and maintain, the reason lies not in our nature, but in an education that has brought us down to a poverty of self-understanding. The fault is not in something we are and, therefore, cannot change, but something we have learned to be and can, therefore, unlearn.

Every individual must learn to bring the antagonistic inclinations and competing motivations of his two natures into one harmonious flow of productive energy to exemplify the general principle that: "Progress is the expression of spirit in the world of matter." [36] Their proper union, far from being a static, inert state is one of great energy in dynamic equilibrium. When accomplished, it creates a win/win situation from seemingly win/lose principles, what Baha'u'llah described as: "converting satanic strength into heavenly power." [37] To accomplish that transformation is the quest for inner harmony, coherence, unity, and truth.

The Quest for Harmony

Spiritual purpose and material purpose can be harmonized, as the natures can, if their proper relations are understood. When the spiritual and material are in harmony the condition of truth is attained and humanity prospers and develops in a sustainable way. But such harmony never makes spirit and matter equal. The spiritual must always remain more important. If the material and the spiritual walk hand-in-hand, it is the spiritual that is the guiding hand. It is like the painter and his paints. Both are necessary for a painting to come into being, but the painter is more important than the paints he uses. Likewise, 'Abdu'l-Bahá aptly said that true civilization is "where the spiritual is expressed and carried out in the material." [38] Reconciling the spiritual and the material is like the painter struggling to embody his vision on canvas. Vision and execution must be in harmony with possibility before realization can occur. No epic poem can be crammed into sonnet form, and a sonnet stretched out to epic length is just sonorous wind.

The quest for harmony is the struggle to bring selfish impulses under spiritual authority. Yet the spiritual self can not bring ego impulses into harmony, so long as it exists only as potential. To work this potential must be activated; else the psychic undertow of ego desires, the sheer gravitational pull of the material world, will overcome the efforts of most people to break free of it. Potential must be actualized. The soul must be assisted to be free of the world.

In looking to answer the question, "Who are you?, we found that while the soul is created good, the individual is not naturally good, but only potentially so. "Good character must be taught," asserted the Master. [39]

This is done by the educative power of the Word of God—i.e. by divine education. Baha'u'llah asserts: "And yet, is not the object of every Revelation to effect a transformation in the whole character of mankind, a transformation that shall manifest itself both outwardly and inwardly, that shall affect both its inner life and external conditions? For if the character of mankind be not changed, the futility of God's universal Manifestations would be apparent." [40]

But the soul must want transformation. There is an indispensable volitional aspect to transformation. Baha'u'llah points out that: "All that which ye potentially possess can, however, be manifested only as a result of your own volition. Your own acts testify to this truth." [41] Thoughts without the will to execute them are mere electrical waves passing through the brain. Hopes for salvation that rely on magical potions like the "blood of the lamb" are still bound to the wheel of dependency. But with volition, a transformational dynamic is released that creates a desire for action and steers it toward a desired end. I mean that to be complete and effective, spiritual impulses must find expression, and expression needs spiritual principles to guide it into altruistic form.

A spiritual principle, such as love thy neighbor as thyself, brings human spiritual potential into actuality because it identifies a certain attitude and behavior as right and proper and motivates people to act that way. It "educes" and shapes some potential that is "immanent" within the human reality. Because spiritual principles harmonize with that which is immanent in human nature they resonate with it, activating its virtues and powers through a sort of vibrational effect, a kind of resonant morphology. But they also harmonize with all in creation and within the human soul since "the universe is enfolded within thee." Through obedience to spiritual principles the weeds of the lower nature are cultivated into the flowers of the higher nature. That is, spiritual principles do not change the painting, but the painter, who then changes his paintings.

There is more to know of human nature than just being subjectively aware of this much, of course, but we need go no further at this point. We will understand more of human nature as we answer the other questions we need to focus upon. For these questions cannot be fully answered independently of each other. We can no more really know ourselves independently of knowing our purpose, or even prior to knowing something of how to act towards others, than we can know our purpose and determine our actions independently of knowing who or what we really are. In one sense, the four questions open up four overlapping contexts of inquiry, each one, on its own level, primarily concerned with one question with the others forming a background landscape, but, from another perspective, they are four doors leading to a common center. The careful reader will not have missed the only half-submerged views about purpose and action that appeared in the just completed discussion about human nature. Nevertheless, there is a certain priority. That is, spiritually we are something before we do anything, and we can act more effectively if we know both why we act and what the proper context of action is. So we had to start with some clear idea of who we are and how to find that out. Then what we should do is easier to determine, though still difficult to do.

Let us go to the second question and ask:

To What Purpose Do We Exist?

We cherish the hope that through the loving-kindness of the All-Wise, the All-Knowing, the obscuring dust may be dispelled and the power of perception enhanced, that the people may discover the purpose for which they have been called into being.
(Bahá'u'lláh, *Tablets of Bahá'u'lláh*, p. 35)

The Guardian of the Bahá'í Faith, Shoghi Effendi, wrote: "The Bahá'í Faith, like all other Divine religions, is thus fundamentally mystic in character. Its chief goal is the development of the individual and society, through the acquisition of spiritual virtues and powers. It is the soul of man that has first to be fed." [1]

While many would agree in the abstract with Shoghi Effendi's statement, it is clear from the state of the world that we don't act on this belief with any real consistency. Why? I believe that in the last few hundred years the leading peoples of the world have lived from primarily a materialistic philosophy. One positive result of this style of life and thought has been an unprecedented material productivity. But we have lost the principle that the soul must first be fed. We don't feed the soul first because we fear losing this comfortable way of life. This is self-centered, and like it or not, we privileged people are losing it anyway. The very success of our economic productivity has generated a thinking that gives undue importance to material life and the values that justify selfishness. Many think money or more material goods alone can solve our economic and psychological problems. That is wrong.

Our True Relation

Bahá'u'lláh's estimation of the value of this world is this: "The world is but a show, vain and empty, a mere nothing, bearing the semblance of reality. Set not your affections upon it. Break not the bond that uniteth you with your Creator, and be not of those that have erred and strayed from His ways. Verily I say, the world is like the vapor in a desert, which the thirsty dreameth to be water and striveth after it with all his might, until when he cometh unto it, he findeth it to be mere illusion. It may, moreover, be likened unto the lifeless image of the beloved whom the lover hath sought and found, in the end, after long search and to his utmost regret, to be such as cannot 'fatten nor appease his hunger'."(2) 'Abdu'l-Bahá echoes His Father's statement: "This present life is even as a swelling wave, or a mirage, or drifting shadows. Could ever a distorted image on the desert serve as refreshing waters? No, by the Lord of Lords! Never can reality and the mere semblance of reality be one, and wide is the difference between fancy and fact, between truth and the phantom thereof." (3)

Material things are real enough, as anyone running into a wall can tell you. So when Bahá'u'lláh says the world is a mere nothing, He does not mean it is not real. He means it is of little value compared to spiritual reality and that the materialistic mind overvalues it. Bahá'u'lláh identifies our true relation with material wealth: "In earthly riches fear is hidden and peril is concealed." (4) He goes on: "Fleeting are the riches of the world; all that perisheth and changeth is not, and hath never been, worthy of attention, except to a recognized measure." (5)

One can never gain security and peace from pursuing, possessing and accumulating material riches because fear and peril are hidden and concealed in their very substance. These dangers are real because material things are always threatening to dissolve or be snatched from us. They are a fleeting form of congealed dust. The reality of material riches is illusion itself, compared to the spiritual. The gold they give is only a fool's gold, material wealth being but the semblance, the simulacra, of inner spiritual riches. Their promise of riches, security and peace is a lie because they can only deliver fear, suspicion and competitive self-interest. The more material riches are pursued and accumulated, whether by individuals or nations, the more fear and a sense of imperilment is brought into human life, for that pursuit is merely chasing shadows and phantoms through the looking glass! But fear and peril are difficult to see because they are hidden beneath the sparkling glitter of allurement—"If I get that big raise I'll...."

The whole materialist paradigm is driven to overcome these paralyzing feelings of loss and fear of poverty by the donkey's carrot of short-sighted pursuit of self-interest and material accumulation. Not only is there no common prosperity there, there can never be any sense of prosperity, for the lower nature is a poverty mentality of anxieties seeking compensation in a lust for power or material security. But no matter how much power or material wealth is acquired, anxiety never goes away, for fear and peril are essential aspects of material things. As we become engaged in cutthroat competition for limited resources we lose any sense of our spiritual nature and become blind to true human purpose.

But some accumulation is necessary for economic life to progress. Accumulation is justified. Without surplus there can be no investment and thus no chance to generate more wealth. But while accumulation is good, disproportionate accumulation by the few is not. Prosperity is founded on social justice and personal generosity. To become truly prosperous and not just materially wealthy, individuals must share and cooperate, not compete and over-accumulate, and society must have laws which support personal and collective virtue. Many say they will altruistically give after they acquire wealth, but this almost never works. Acquisitiveness breeds not altruism but more acquisitiveness. Thus the more one has the more one wants, for one never feels prosperous.

Hoarding and over-accumulation oppose all the spiritual virtues. They even oppose the reality of material wealth, which is whatever is circulating and thus doing work or is saved as potential for work. Active wealth is what is in circulation, like blood throughout the body. Material wealth is the life-blood of society. The reason, then, for some accumulation is as a storehouse of energy for future work, or to get through lean times: the "saving for a rainy day" principle.

In proper measure, material desires and purpose are a necessary part of human life and well-being. But materialism as a philosophy is built entirely on fiction and illusion, for all material poverty generates anxiety which fuels a compensating avariciousness. From prolonged exposure to this illusion, to this improper education that brings forth ego-qualities, we have bought into the delusion given us.

Shoghi Effendi puts it this way: "Indeed the chief reason for the evils now rampant in society is the lack of spirituality. The materialistic civilization of our age has so much absorbed the energy and interest of mankind that people in general do no longer feel the necessity of raising themselves above the forces and conditions of their daily material existence. There is not sufficient demand for things that we call spiritual to differentiate them from the needs and requirements of our physical existence.

The universal crisis affecting mankind is, therefore, essentially spiritual in its causes. The spirit of the age, taken on the whole, is irreligious. Man's outlook on life is too crude and materialistic to enable him to elevate himself into the higher realms of the spirit." [6]

Inner poverty can only be assuaged by spiritual riches, not by more material wealth. The real scarcity today is within our empty souls, not in our lighter pocketbooks. We don't see this, or only see it through a heavy fog of confused thoughts, because our value system, as it is called, is horribly skewed. We have an ego-based morality. So we overvalue material riches when they should not be considered "except to a recognized measure". We overvalue the body, when "the reality of man is his thought." [7] We overvalue competition and fight with ferocious self-interest yet "all were made for harmony and union." With these barriers to spiritual and social advance firmly entrenched we lock ourselves within a poverty mentality and see no way out of this prison except to try harder to produce material plenty and then to keep most of it for ourselves. We resemble exhausted lab rats running on a wheel, going nowhere, but maintaining the belief that if we only run faster or smarter the next time around we'll grasp the ring. But the wheel only goes around faster and we are further exhausted. Finally, some may understand, there is no ring to grasp. The wheel turns by our running and it is smarter to give up than be chewed up.

In viewing our proper relationship with material wealth Bahá'u'lláh again presents a view opposed to the common one: "Thou dost wish for gold and I desire thy freedom from it. Thou thinkest thyself rich in its possession, and I recognize thy wealth in thy sanctity therefrom." [8] So that we may be educated to see ourselves and the world properly the divine Educator warns: "Busy not thyself with this world, for with fire We test the gold, and with gold We test Our servants." [9] We are finding out that the attraction for gold, or material wealth, is a spiritual fire we put our souls in—and it can roast the spirit.

But Baha'u'llah's warnings about gold cannot mean "be poor and have nothing to do with improving the world". There is no inherent virtue in poverty. Often the "virtues" of the poor are merely the result of the lack of means and opportunity to act like the well-to-do at their worst. Baha'u'llah is saying, I believe, that if one is materially wealthy, don't be attached to this wealth. There is no harm or danger in material wealth provided the proper attitude toward it is held. "Should a man," He writes, 'wish to adorn himself with the ornaments of the earth, to wear its apparels, or partake of the benefits it can bestow, no harm can befall him, if he alloweth nothing whatever to intervene between him and God, for God hath ordained every good thing, whether created in the heavens or in the earth, for such of His servants as truly believe in Him. Eat ye, O people, of the good things which God hath allowed you, and deprive not yourselves from His wondrous bounties." [10]

Our real wealth is within, since we are created rich. Pursuing material wealth in itself is always a tricky affair. It becomes a real problem when means become ends in themselves, when wealth "in itself" morphs into wealth "for itself." Attachment is always dependence, which is poverty-thinking. Attachment is the barrier, not gold itself. It is not the soft, yellow metal that is a test, but the soft allurements that gold represents in terms of personal privilege, power, influence and security. But often we don't know of our attachments until the threat of losing what we are attached to arises. If attachment to the wish for gold is the test, then the poor, too, must be detached from this wish, or they will be, psychologically, the same as the rich. The actual relationship of wealth and poverty in this world is cyclical: "If poverty overtake thee, be not sad; for in time the Lord of wealth shall visit thee. Fear not abasement, for glory shall one day rest on thee." [11] And: "Be not troubled in poverty nor confident in riches, for poverty is followed by riches, and riches are followed by poverty." [12]

Yet however many times we may have ridden the hobbyhorse of anxiety and frustration that is material attachments, we will still pretty consistently try it again. Why such a slow learning curve? Part of the problem is the twin self-serving attitudes that often accompany the successful pursuit of material wealth. If wealth is seen as the result of intelligence, enterprise and hard work, then misfortune, little or no education, and lack of opportunity are seen as products of bad character. This is called blaming the victim, and blind ideologues use it to justify punishing the sick and the poor. But wide-spread poverty is neither crime nor character flaw, but the result of structural inequalities in the social system; inequalities that are stoutly defended and rationalized by the privileged. This must change.

Until such time as these structures are fixed, there is a way off the merry-go-round of poverty/wealth//wealth/poverty: "Yet to be poor in all save God is a wondrous gift, belittle not the value thereof, for in the end it will make thee rich in God, and thus thou shalt know the meaning of the utterance, 'In truth ye are the poor,' and the holy words, 'God is the all-possessing,' shall even as the true morn break forth gloriously resplendent upon the horizon of the lover's heart, and abide secure on the throne of wealth." **(13)** In another place Baha'u'llah asks: "What advantage is there in a life that can be overtaken by death, or in an existence that is doomed to extinction, or in a prosperity that is subject to change?" **(14)** The only possible advantage is one that brings advantage to all.

Human Purposes

The Bahá'í Writings state that human life has many purposes, because we live in different spiritual and social contexts. Learning these purposes connects with the educative purposes of the Manifestations. Foremost among all human purposes, perhaps, is to achieve eternal life. On the education side: "The Prophets and Messengers of God have been sent down for the sole purpose of guiding mankind to the straight Path of Truth. The purpose underlying Their revelation hath been to educate all men, that they may, at the hour of death, ascend, in the utmost purity and sanctity and with absolute detachment, to the throne of the Most High." **(15)**

Now, in an essay on earthly prosperity one might rightly wonder what this other-worldly purpose has to do with anything: actually, quite a bit. 'Abdu'l-Baha says there is a direct connection between this purpose and social action for common prosperity. He states: "…we must be the servants of the poor, helpers of the poor, remember the sorrows of the poor, associate with them; for thereby we may inherit the Kingdom of heaven." **(16)** In his treatise, *The Secret of Divine Civilization*, He wrote that "the primary purpose in revealing the Divine Law…is to bring about happiness in the after life and civilization and the refinement of character in this." **(17)**

Regarding refinement of character, 'Abdu'l-Bahá says that another purpose is to acquire virtues. To refine character is to improve and beautify our thought and behavior, and to more perfectly manifest human potentials. This returns us to last chapter's discussion about immensely rich souls, who are, nonetheless, poor and needy. Spiritually, we are created rich in potentials; a talisman with a whole universe of riches enfolded within. To be poor and needy, then, does not refer to any inherent lack of spiritual riches, but to be poor and needy in spiritual knowledge. To provide humanity with that knowledge and the drive to acquire it is why the Manifestations come. A diamond buried in a mine is only potential wealth. It must be mined, cut and polished for that potential to be made actual. The soul is a mine rich in gems: rich, that is, in all save God.

Similarly, to acquire virtues means learning the skills, knowledge, techniques and practices that enable us to "bring forth" the gems deposited in the mine of the human spirit "so that mankind may benefit therefrom." To fully achieve this lofty goal, however, the character which the soul acquires from education must itself be suffused with divine virtue. We receive physical and mental instruction from secular education, but unless education also has the divine Word it will not bring forth our virtue, but, rather, deprive us of what we inherently possess, for the individual must develop physically, intellectually, and morally to be complete.

Acquiring virtues is what is known as moral or spiritual transformation. Transformation is personal effort responding to the supernatural power of the Word of God. Knowledge alone is not sufficient. Transformation cannot occur absent the soul's "labor" to "translate that which hath been written into reality and action." [18]

Thus this purpose connects directly with the purpose of God in creating human beings and relating them to Himself, through His Manifestations. Bahá'u'lláh wrote: "The Purpose of the one true God, exalted be His glory, in revealing Himself unto men is to lay bare those gems that lie hidden within the mine of their true and inmost selves." [19] We must neither squander nor bury these gifts, as the Biblical parable of the talents also warns. Bahá'u'lláh also admonishes: "Be not careless of the virtues with which ye have been endowed, neither be neglectful of your high destiny." [20] But we must no longer allow "improper education" to deprive us of them, either.

The Grace of God

Another human purpose Bahá'u'lláh states as: "The whole duty of man in this Day is to attain that share of the flood of grace which God poureth forth for him. Let none, therefore, consider the largeness or smallness of the receptacle." [21] What is the grace of God? In my view, in its broadest sense the grace of God is His Message, the historical revelation of the invisible and eternal truth. Baha'u'llah says the Word of God "is God's all-pervasive grace, from which all grace doth emanate." [22] This all-pervasive grace gets particularized in each person. St. Paul helps us understand this when he writes of: "Having then gifts differing according to the grace that is given to us…" [23]

Regardless of our circumstances, grace becomes active in our lives when we exert ourselves to receive it. "Please God, the poor may exert themselves and strive to earn the means of livelihood. This is a duty which, in this most great Revelation, hath been prescribed unto every one, and is accounted in the sight of God as a goodly deed. Whoso observeth this duty, the help of the invisible One shall most certainly aid him. He can enrich, through His grace, whomsoever He pleaseth. He, verily, hath power over all things...." [24] We are back to knowing our inner spiritual capital as those innate gifts or gems deposited within, and striving to realize this potential in our outer lives.

Advancing Civilization

Another purpose is to "carry forward an ever-advancing civilization." [25] I don't wish too stray into this discussion on the social level, for that would get us into an examination of the institutions of the Divine Economy, and this essay is really limited to a discussion of spiritual education. Suffice it to say, that in my opinion social institutions everywhere and at every level will no doubt evolve and become more humane as they buckle, then crumble, then are rebuilt in new global form by wise leaders of humankind under the imperative of manifesting the oneness of humanity.

However, before that civilization becomes a reality that we live within and not just dream about, every individual has still two important roles to play in the moral economy in advancing civilization toward that goal.

First, while most individuals can only negligibly advance material civilization, every person can play a central role in advancing spiritual civilization and the moral economy by acting as a model of moral behavior. The Universal House of Justice pointed out: "The light of the Revelation is destined to illumine every sphere of endeavor; in each, the relationships that sustain society are to be recast; in each, the world seeks examples of how human beings should be to one another. We offer for your consideration, given its conspicuous part in generating ferment in which so many people have recently been embroiled, the economic life of humanity, where injustice is tolerated with indifference and disproportionate gain is regarded as the emblem of success. So deeply entrenched are such pernicious attitudes that it is hard to imagine how any one individual can alone alter the prevailing standards by which the relationships in this domain are governed. Nevertheless, there are certainly practices a Bahá'í would eschew, such as dishonesty in one's transactions or the economic exploitation of others. Faithful adherence to the divine admonitions demands there be no contradiction between one's economic conduct and one's beliefs as a Baha'i. By applying in one's life those principles of the Faith that relate to fairness and equity, a single soul can uphold a standard far above the low threshold by which the world measures itself. Humanity is weary for want of a pattern of life to which to aspire." (26)

In the moral economy, a prosperous enterprise not only generates material profit, but also helps to build moral capacity within all levels of the work community. Rank and file workers no less than corporate leaders can model ethical principles and thus foster the development of the moral environment. The workplace is not only a place to earn wages, produce goods and services, and engage in material exchange. It must also be the place where individuals may learn and freely express qualities such as truthfulness, compassion and generosity. Making spiritual development one of the primary goals of work and professional life constitutes a revolution in organization and purposes of work, and in the perception of wealth and riches.[27]

Lest we think such action has only limited or no effect, consider this promise from Bahá'u'lláh: "Whoso ariseth, in this Day, to aid Our Cause, and summoneth to his assistance the hosts of a praiseworthy character and upright conduct, the influence flowing from such an action will, most certainly, be diffused throughout the whole world." [28] Advancing spiritual civilization through the power of noble example raises the general consciousness of humanity's spiritual nature: it is the divine reality within each person recognizing and responding to its expression in the actions of others. Uplifting human consciousness subtly influences society and people toward ends that benefit everybody.

The second role to be played in advancing civilization is through one's actual labor, especially if that work is in answer to a felt calling. To work and labor is itself an essential need of human beings, for creativity is a fundamental drive of the human reality. This need to work is not a poverty need of the ego, but, rather, a spiritual need flowing out from inherent riches, the need to find productive expression of inborn gifts and talents. The Bahá'í teachings state: "Genuine wealth is created when work is undertaken not simply as a means of earning a livelihood but also as a way to contribute to society. We hold that meaningful work is a basic need of the human soul, as important to the proper development of the individual as nutritious food, clean water and fresh air are to the physical body." [29]

I said earlier that Baha'u'llah's warnings about gold cannot mean, "be poor" or, "have nothing to do with improving the world". Proper work of any kind is the way that every individual improves society by adding to its common wealth. Hence, Baha'u'llah admonishes that to have a livelihood "is a duty which, in this most great Revelation, hath been prescribed unto every one." Its personal benefit is brought out in another of His injunctions: "(I)t is incumbent on every one to engage in crafts and professions, for therein lies the secret of wealth, O men of understanding!" [30] And the relation between livelihood and divine powers to achieve personal destiny is explained in this counsel to an individual: "Concerning the means of livelihood, thou shouldst, while placing thy whole trust in God, engage in some occupation. He will assuredly send down upon thee from the heaven of His favour that which is destined for thee. He is in truth the God of might and power." [31]

It is in this same light of purpose that we can examine Baha'u'llah's statement: "It is enjoined upon every one of you to engage in some form of occupation, such as crafts, trades and the like." [32] Although He enjoins everyone "to engage in some form of occupation, such as crafts, trades and the like", it should be clear that we are not being admonished simply to go find a job, though for many that is the only possible employ. But work of any kind is really about personal spiritual growth and social advancement.

The document, *The Prosperity of Humankind*, points out: "In most of contemporary thinking, the concept of work has been largely reduced to that of gainful employment aimed at acquiring the means for the consumption of available goods. The system is circular: acquisition and consumption resulting in the maintenance and expansion of the production of goods and, in consequence, in supporting paid employment. Taken individually, all of these activities are essential to the well-being of society. The inadequacy of the overall conception, however, can be read in both the apathy that social commentators discern among large numbers of the employed in every land and the demoralization of the growing armies of the unemployed....Not surprisingly, therefore, there is increasing recognition that the world is in urgent need of a new "work ethic." [33]

A strong work ethic is an intrinsic part of the emerging moral economy. Shoghi Effendi wrote apropos this theme: "It is the duty of those who are in charge of the organization of society to give every individual the opportunity of acquiring the necessary talent in some kind of profession, and also the means of utilizing such a talent, both for its own sake and for the sake of earning the means of his livelihood. Every individual, no matter how handicapped and limited he may be, is under the obligation of engaging in some work or profession, for work, specially when performed in the spirit of service, is according to Bahá'u'lláh a form of worship. It has not only a utilitarian purpose, but has a value in itself, because it draws us nearer to God, and enables us to better grasp His purpose for us in this world." (34)

Part of Shoghi Effendi's statement pointed to the spiritual aspect of work, as stated by Baha'u'llah: "We have graciously exalted your engagement in such work to the rank of worship unto God, the True One. Ponder ye in your hearts the grace and the blessings of God and render thanks unto Him at eventide and at dawn." (35) 'Abdu'l-Baha further elucidates this most important theme: "The man who makes a piece of notepaper to the best of his ability, conscientiously, concentrating all his forces on perfecting it, is giving praise to God. Briefly, all effort and exertion put forth by man from the fullness of his heart is worship, if it is prompted by the highest motives and the will to do service to humanity. This is worship: to serve mankind and to minister to the needs of the people. Service is prayer. A physician ministering to the sick, gently, tenderly, free from prejudice and believing in the solidarity of the human race, he is giving praise." (36)

Working in a spirit of worship is to constantly renew the force which enables human beings to both grow spiritually and to advance materially. To think of "pay" only in terms of wages is clearly obsolete in such a framework. There are higher kinds of pay: gaining a sense of purpose; increasing personal dignity, respect, and honor; and feeling one is contributing to community life in a productive manner. To be spiritually fulfilling, human labor must serve some end greater than personal monetary gain or social advantage. The social purpose of work is service to the common good. Good work attitudes will not be evoked by higher wages alone, but educed through expression and demonstration of noble values. The decent moral life can not depend upon material comfort, for that will quickly crumble when comfort is threatened.

So important is work for personal and social development that Baha'u'llah warns: "The most despised of men in the sight of God are those who sit idly and beg. Hold ye fast unto the cord of material means, placing your whole trust in God, the Provider of all means." [37] On the other side of the social scale, lest the rich believe their wealth exempts them from working, Shoghi Effendi states: "It is obvious, therefore, that the inheritance of wealth cannot make anyone immune from daily work." [38] Of course, work can be interpreted here very broadly and does not necessarily mean "going to the office."

In the Bahá'í teachings, spiritual development is never presented as the outcome of some special practices divorced from the practical activities of this world. This world and the next are directly connected, and what goes on "here" has effects "there." The reverse is also true. Thus work itself is a spiritual practice, when seen as a form of worship. Those gifted in their work are blessed. Baha'u'llah advises us to "treat craftsmen with deference..." [39] and says: "Great indeed is the claim of scientists and craftsmen on the peoples of the world." [40]

The social influence and status that comes with receiving deference should not be used by scientists, artists and craftsmen only for their personal gain or advantage, but also to improve the general good. Baha'u'llah wrote in this regard: "The purpose of learning should be the promotion of the welfare of the people, and this can be achieved through crafts. It hath been revealed and is now repeated that the true worth of artists and craftsmen should be appreciated, for they advance the affairs of mankind." [41]

Work of any kind done with dignity, integrity and as service is honorable, but, beyond all this, individuals are, I believe, admonished to look for and spiritual education should help them find something else. Though all work is good when undertaken with sincere intent to grow and serve, there is a specific kind of work each person should try to find. This work is the inner secret of the secret of wealth, so to speak. This purpose is explicitly stated by Bahá'u'lláh: "The best of men are they that earn a livelihood by their calling and spend upon themselves and upon their kindred for the love of God, the Lord of all worlds." (42)

"True reliance," He says, "is for the servant to pursue his profession and calling in this world, to hold fast unto the Lord, to seek naught but His grace, inasmuch as in His Hands is the destiny of all His servants." (43) Thus every soul is not only created, but also is created, I believe, to fulfill a destined purpose. The first signs of a calling are those natural abilities, interests and aptitudes in, say, athletics, art, science, scholarship, or trade, which education can help the student identify and develop. These are demonstrated in one's instinctual aptitudes, often in what one daydreams about. Such abilities and dreams are indicators of a life path. What do you like to do? What are you almost instinctively good at? The poet, Rumi, said: "Everyone has been made for some particular work, and the desire for that work has been put in every heart." The Buddha is reported to have stated: "Your work is to discover your work and then, with all your heart, to give yourself to it." Knowing this desire as a call from God to lead you back to Him in occupation is also part of self-knowledge.

But individual purpose is not realized solely by focusing on what one feels one is created to do, but also on what one is created to give. These are two sides of the same coin. That is, the created to do and created to serve purposes should be inseparable. Each individual is created to do something, which he or she feels called to do, but that individual is, from a spiritual point of view, then required, if he is to fully achieve his purpose, to contribute that something to the common wealth through service. In a nutshell, our goal is to find our calling, but our purpose is to serve. Hence one purpose in knowing ourselves is to understand how we can serve most effectively.

Any job, craft or profession can bring remuneration, of course, and one can serve humanity from any place in the work force. But there seems to be a special magic in pursuing one's calling by giving an affirmative response to the divine call to occupation "put in every heart." Such a fortunate one will experience a tremendous release of energy and imagination that endures a lifetime. 'Abdu'l-Baha made this wonderful statement connecting higher impulses, exuberant feeling, practical expression, and finding the right path: "Joy gives us wings! In times of joy our strength is more vital, our intellect keener, and our understanding less clouded. We seem better able to cope with the world and to find our sphere of usefulness. But when sadness visits us we become weak, our strength leaves us, our comprehension is dim and our intelligence veiled. The actualities of life seem to elude our grasp, the eyes of our spirits fail to discover the sacred mysteries, and we become even as dead beings." (44) Fulfilling one's calling is a powerful way to shape an uncertain destiny into a more certain future.

The lucky among us learn that a good way to find wealth is through using our innate gifts to pursue a calling. But the best of us know that, like wealth, our innate gifts are not for hoarding or for self-indulgence, but to help humankind. The spiritually mature person could never use personal wealth only for himself while others were in deprivation. Rather, he would see the possession of material wealth as a gift to use responsibly to alleviate to whatever extent possible the distress of those in need around him or, more generally, through larger charities and humanitarian organizations. To him it is inconceivable that those who have plenty would not provide for those who have naught. That is, he would act as the grace of God for others.

It is in this light that we can ponder the following quote from 'Abdu'l-Baha, part of which was quoted earlier: "Wealth is most commendable, provided the entire population is wealthy. If, however, a few have inordinate riches while the rest are impoverished, and no fruit or benefit accrues from that wealth, then it is only a liability to its possessor. If, on the other hand, it is expended for the promotion of knowledge, the founding of elementary and other schools, the encouragement of art and industry, the training of orphans and the poor —in brief, if it is dedicated to the welfare of society—its possessor will stand out before God and man as the most excellent of all who live on earth and will be accounted as one of the people of paradise." (45)

I have attempted till now in this discussion on the purposes in our lives to link it with the notion of prosperity as the balance between material wealth and spiritual riches in one's personal life and interpersonal relations, with some quick side-glances at larger social contexts. That is, the moral economy, poised between the spiritual and the material, the eternal and the contingent, blends characteristics of both realms. Thus the discussion went from discovering the material aspect of achieving eternal life to unveiling the spiritual aspect of daily human work. Maturity brings these purposes together into one comprehensive purpose, and the personal gives way to the social which becomes primary. Maturity, as we will see, is a special time, one fraught with dangers, but also replete with opportunity.

Maturity: The Great Divide

We start with the following statement: "The first Taraz and the first effulgence which hath dawned from the horizon of the Mother Book is that man should know his own self and recognize that which leadeth unto loftiness or lowliness, glory or abasement, wealth or poverty. Having attained the stage of fulfillment and reached his maturity, man standeth in need of wealth, and such wealth as he acquireth through crafts or professions is commendable and praiseworthy in the estimation of men of wisdom, and especially in the eyes of servants who dedicate themselves to the education of the world and to the edification of its peoples." (46)

The key phrase for us here is "having attained the stage of fulfillment and reached his maturity, man standeth in need of wealth." Bahá'u'lláh defines maturity as recognizing what leads to loftiness or lowliness, glory or abasement, wealth or poverty, and acting consistently on this knowledge. Maturity is a condition of wisdom, when the spiritual essence comes forth because it is well supported both bodily and psychologically. Similarly, the process of social development leading to maturity is, ideally anyway, the process of building the outer social vessel that can receive the full flow of spiritual energy from Revelation. Maturity is marked by the harmonizing of our conflicting natures, at whatever age that is accomplished. This occurs through proper spiritual education. Bahá'u'lláh explains: "Man is even as steel, the essence of which is hidden: through admonition and explanation, good counsel and education, the essence will be brought to light. If, however, he be allowed to remain in his original condition, the corrosion of lusts and appetites will effectively destroy him." (47)

Why after maturity is wealth needed? 'Abdu'l-Bahá is reported to have said: "Provided they behave moderately, the more people advance in the material realm, the more their capacity for spirituality is augmented. The sounder the body, the greater the resplendency and manifestation of the spirit." (48) While the expression of spirituality can be augmented by material wealth, spirituality is not dependent upon material wealth, of course. Material wealth can be the greatest barrier to spirit. Hence material poverty can be a stimulus for spirituality. 'Abdu'l-Baha explained that: "Spiritual conditions are not dependent upon the possession of worldly treasures or the absence of them. When physically destitute, spiritual thoughts are more likely. Poverty is stimulus toward God."(49) Nonetheless, inner spiritual quality always needs a support in the outer material world to be properly manifest and effective. This support is not a passive receptacle of energies, but the means of extending the influence of the inner quality, of giving it social force and power, and to call forth greater pulsations of this inner power from the inexhaustible Source. It is like a light reflected in a clear mirror that becomes "light upon light."

At the stage of fulfillment and maturity there should occur a great but almost indefinable transformation in one's purpose. There should be a turn of life from self-centered to self-sacrificing, and a change from seeing wealth as the means to enrich "me first" to a means for the development and security of "you-before-me". Baha'u'llah states: "Blessed is he who preferreth his brother before himself." (50) This change itself is perhaps the true definition of the state of maturity. It is no less true for individual possessing wealth, than it is for the whole class of the wealthy, and great are the heavenly rewards for those who achieve this spiritual maturity. Their honor is tied to the great honor of the patient poor. Baha'u'llah admonishes: "They who are possessed of riches, however, must have the utmost regard for the poor, for great is the honor destined by God for those poor who are steadfast in patience. By My life! There is no honor, except what God may please to bestow, that can compare to this honor. Great is the blessedness awaiting the poor that endure patiently and conceal their sufferings, and well is it with the rich who bestow their riches on the needy and prefer them before themselves." (51) This statement alone sheds a powerful light that illuminates the inner dynamic of the moral economy of sharing, service and self-sacrifice.

How an individual uses his material wealth is one indicator of how spiritually mature he really is. If he wishes to decide his actions from the lower or ego nature, his activities will be given over almost exclusively to pursuing privilege, money, personal influence or other means of private gain and advantage. Many never outgrow these pursuits. It can even be said that materialistic civilization, in general, is stuck at this level. Though there is nothing inherently wrong with most ego desires at their proper level of human development, the danger is that there can be no end to them, and so one never gets to the business of spiritual growth. On the ego level, too, one encounters others with the same kind of goals and these might counteract, overcome, or neutralize your own. In other words, they might get there first, leaving you alone in a "me-first" world with nothing but shattered dreams and empty hopes, nursing thoughts of revenge or despair. At such times 'Abdu'l-Bahá's gentle warning can have effect: "It is indeed a good and praiseworthy thing to progress materially, but in so doing, let us not neglect the more important spiritual progress, and close our eyes to the Divine light shining in our midst." (52)

Maturity, then, is not just reaching one's full physical stature. It is a hard-won experiential understanding and expression of our spiritual nature. Maturity is, for many, the great divide of human consciousness, when narrow self-interest turns to wide selfless interest. Maturity is that state when one knows not only who one is but also what one should be doing and how to accomplish it. Maturity knows that: "Honesty, virtue, wisdom and a saintly character redound to the exaltation of man, while dishonesty, imposture, ignorance and hypocrisy lead to his abasement. By My life! Man's distinction lieth not in ornaments or wealth, but rather in virtuous behaviour and true understanding." (53)

Further, in relation to wealth, the mature soul understands that real wealth is whatever one contributes to the common good, whether in the form of philanthropy, opportunity, knowledge, experience, social service or a shoulder to cry on. "For, it is by contributing to the common good that an individual acquires true spiritual maturity." (54)

The spiritual influence generated by sharing material wealth can be most fully expressed at maturity, for the altruistic person can, through philanthropic and charitable acts, by founding schools and hospitals, or financing small businesses, do far more good with his or her wealth than those not so blessed. Again, there are rewards for the giver. Baha'u'llah wrote: "Charity is pleasing and praiseworthy in the sight of God and is regarded as a prince among goodly deeds. Consider ye and call to mind that which the All-Merciful hath revealed in the Qur'án: 'They prefer them before themselves, though poverty be their own lot. And with such as are preserved from their own covetousness shall it be well.' Viewed in this light, the blessed utterance above is, in truth, the day-star of utterances. Blessed is he who preferreth his brother before himself. Verily, such a man is reckoned, by virtue of the Will of God, the All-Knowing, the All-Wise, with the people of Baha who dwell in the Crimson Ark." (55) In another place He wrote: "Beware lest ye encroach upon the substance of your neighbor. Prove yourselves worthy of his trust and confidence in you, and withhold not from the poor the gifts which the grace of God hath bestowed upon you. He, verily, shall recompense the charitable, and doubly repay them for what they have bestowed. No God is there but Him. All creation and its empire are His. He bestoweth His gifts on whom He will, and from whom He will He withholdeth them. He is the Great Giver, the Most Generous, the Benevolent." (56) And finally: "Deal not treacherously with the substance of your neighbor. Be ye trustworthy on earth, and withhold not from the poor the things given unto you by God through His grace. He, verily, will bestow upon you the double of what ye possess. He, in truth, is the All-Bounteous, the Most Generous." (57)

In sum, we can say that every individual has four main purposes: first, to attain eternal life; secondly, to acquire virtues, which means to express innate powers; thirdly, to attain a share of the grace of God, which is also connected with developing innate talents and abilities; and, finally, to advance civilization by engaging in work, being a good moral example, and striving to realize one's calling. These are not separate but rather intimately connected purposes that flow from self-knowledge. They should come together at maturity, and in a sense actually define that condition. Now that we know something of human purpose and how it is intimately linked with knowledge of our true self we can go to the third question:

How Should We Act Towards One Another?

God grant that all men may turn unto the treasures latent within their own beings.
(Tablets of Baha'u'llah: 72)

We are learning the hard way that real happiness resides neither in a mad, frenetic pursuit of material things, nor in that drowsy complacency resulting from gorging on a glut of goods, or rather it may for awhile, but it cannot endure without developing our virtues, both private and public. We are slowly and painfully returning to an understanding that sees the universe and Reality itself as essentially a spiritual creation not a material mechanism.

The evolution of what has become a materialist order of life, thought, and society was built upon an ethos of self-interest at every level, from the individual to the nation. 'Abdu'l-Baha summed up that ethos this way: "Today, all the peoples of the world are indulging in self-interest and exert the utmost effort and endeavour to promote their own material interests. They are worshipping themselves and not the divine reality, nor the world of mankind. They seek diligently their own benefit and not the common weal. This is because they are captives of the world of nature and unaware of the divine teachings, of the bounty of the Kingdom and of the Sun of Truth." [1]

Opposed to this self-centered ethic that is anarchic, competitive and divisive, Baha'u'llah asserts the moral view that has animated every great religion: "Forget your own selves, and turn your eyes towards your neighbor. Bend your energies to whatever may foster the education of men." **(2)** And: "Do not busy yourselves in your own concerns; let your thoughts be fixed upon that which will rehabilitate the fortunes of mankind and sanctify the hearts and souls of men." **(3)** Comparing the value of the inner gems of virtue to the outer material wealth, He asserts: "Were ye to discover the hidden, the shoreless oceans of My incorruptible wealth, ye would, of a certainty, esteem as nothing the world, nay, the entire creation." **(4)**

I have said that one purpose is to acquire virtues. Acquire means, as we saw, to bring forth into manifest reality the innate powers lying within us by learning from the divine Word how to draw them forth. Hence, 'Abdu'l-Baha exhorts: "Strive as much as ye can to turn wholly toward the Kingdom, that ye may acquire innate courage and ideal power." **(5)** But we also learned that to bring forth the moral gems requires the supernatural power of the Word of God, the divine Educator, and models of these virtues in action by others.

What are some of the personal virtues needed to solve our economic problem?

Personal Virtues of Prosperity

I am going to put forward what I call the ten personal virtues of prosperity. These virtues are gem-like potentialities of "inestimable value" that have been deposited within every human being and which proper education nurtures and develops. These gems of virtue are not like set-in-stone gems, however, mere adornments to a pious life. They are powers not verbal platitudes, vibrating fields of inner power, resonant, talismanic charms that enable us to attract assistance from the spiritual realm whenever we "spend" them caring for others. Practicing them releases their powers and helps to create prosperity. 'Abdu'l-Baha states this theme most effectively, and in the context of spiritual education: "Education must be considered as most important, for as diseases in the world of bodies are extremely contagious, so, in the same way, qualities of spirit and heart are extremely contagious." (6) We are, it seems, hardwired, perhaps via mirror neurons, to be virtuous. Recall that Baha'u'llah said that "all were made for harmony and union."

Virtues, then, are the right and proper way for human beings to behave toward each other. They are templates for morally effective action. The reward they bestow is both intrinsic and extrinsic. Being inherent potentialities in our higher, essential nature their reward is intrinsic in that their proper expression brings feelings of confidence, joy and well-being. But these powers are extrinsic to our lower nature, since they are trainers and civilizers of that nature and bring to it the kind of things it wants, though often not in the way it believes. By beholding their expression in some people, for example, in parents, others can recognize their own divine nature. Virtues build human relationships on a firm and loving foundation of mutual service. Virtues attract the divinity of others and evoke a spiritual response from them. But there must be those willing to model these virtues: to be the catalyst.

As we can learn to reconcile our two natures into one person, we can also reconcile the two forms of wealth into one. This creates prosperity, for we are then in a state of unity and truth, because inner and outer goals and purposes are harmonized. Again, we are created rich, born into and inheritors of great spiritual wealth. We know, too, how to create material wealth by investing capital and organizing work production, and with the technological revolution of the last two hundred years, the means exist to produce wealth for all beyond the dreams of past kings. The pieces of real prosperity, then, exist, in my opinion. But what is lacking at this juncture is the moral sensibility that spiritual education develops through its emphasis upon the principle of the oneness of humanity. That principle will not find proper expression so long as a consumer culture and mentality dominate our thought. Why?

One of the revolutions spawned by the industrial revolution was a psychological transformation in economics from supply to demand as the drive of material production. For millennia supply limited demand, but the heady promise driving industrial production was that people no longer need place any limit on desire. Demand now drives supply and continuous advances in science and technology are supposed to deliver on that promise. This is the false promise of consumer culture. The promise is false for two reasons. Firstly, it is false because the earth does not contain enough nonrenewable natural resources to produce unlimited material plenty for everyone wanting a share in a global consumer economy. But, secondly, the promise of wealth generates the same dreams of perpetual prosperity among late-comers to consumerism as it did to the early risers, and this dream now perishes on the rocky reality of contradictory psychological pulls.

That is, unfettered desire stimulates both a growing global demand for material resources and a commensurate fear and anxiety among the already well-to-do to keep the levers of power and wealth in their hands. The early birds fight to keep their lifestyle and put forward self-serving reasons why they should keep it and others should not pursue it. These reasons boil down to: "There is not enough for you to have as much as we have. Your desires threaten our privileged lifestyle. You can't have it, unless you take it from us by force!"

Through spiritual education humanity can learn to increase wealth by investing its innate moral capital and organizing the creation and distribution of material wealth upon spiritual principles. A proper distribution of the world's wealth will augment human collective spirituality as it does individual spirituality, and this collective spiritual advance will lead to even better social productivity based upon the sharing of wealth and opportunity. Having realized material prosperity for some, we must now go into a higher realm of virtue to ensure wealth and real prosperity for all. I believe that through the power of magnetically-charged spiritual energy flowing through the practice of virtues individuals can positively influence the whole economic arena of life.

Some may question my choice of virtues: "What, only these virtues and not others?" or, "Why did he not include...."? My answer is that I have found this approach a useful one and I hope the reader does also. It is comprehensive but not overly complex. If any reader wishes to add to or subtract from the list, fine, for they are, naturally, free to make their own list using other virtues. The goal, though, is neither to make lists, nor to argue over whose list is better, but to practice virtues.

The personal virtues that follow derive from the central pivot of Baha'u'llah's teachings, which is the consciousness of the oneness of humanity. That is, these virtues come out of and support that central ideal and give it varied expression in interpersonal relations. They do not have real power without the larger context provided by that consciousness. This must be kept in mind, or they become but separate, disembodied concepts.

First is love. 'Abdu'l-Bahá explained the connection between love and true economics: "The fundamentals of the whole economic condition are divine in nature and are associated with the world of the heart and spirit....Hearts must be so cemented together, love must become so dominant that the rich shall most willingly extend assistance to the poor and take steps to establish these economic adjustments permanently. If it is accomplished in this way, it will be most praiseworthy because then it will be for the sake of God and in the pathway of His service. For example, it will be as if the rich inhabitants of a city should say, 'It is neither just nor lawful that we should possess great wealth while there is abject poverty in this community,' and then willingly give their wealth to the poor, retaining only as much as will enable them to live comfortably.

Strive, therefore, to create love in the hearts in order that they may become glowing and radiant. When that love is shining, it will permeate other hearts even as this electric light illumines its surroundings. When the love of God is established, everything else will be realized. This is the true foundation of all economics....Economic questions will not attract hearts. The love of God alone will attract them. Economic questions are most interesting; but the power which moves, controls and attracts the hearts of men is the love of God." [7]

But this love is no mere benign acceptance of things as they are. It is divine love, and this dynamic power fundamentally and often rapidly changes human conditions. Without love there is only tolerance of differences, without unity there is only passive acceptance of what is. To repeat a statement from 'Abdu'l-Bahá: "See ye no strangers; rather see all men as friends, for love and unity come hard when ye fix your gaze on otherness." "Love is a light that never dwelleth in a heart possessed by fear," says Bahá'u'lláh, [8] bringing to mind the admonition to give "undeterred by the fear of poverty."

But to get a real sense of the power of love let us ponder these words of 'Abdu'l-Baha: "Love is...the vital bond inherent, in accordance with the divine creation, in the realities of things. .... the unique power that bindeth together the divers elements of this material world, the supreme magnetic force that directeth the movements of the spheres in the celestial realms. Love revealeth with unfailing and limitless power the mysteries latent in the universe. Love is the spirit of life unto the adorned body of mankind, the establisher of true civilization in this mortal world, and the shedder of imperishable glory upon every high-aiming race and nation." [9]

Second is truthfulness; "Truthfulness is the foundation of all the virtues of the world of humanity. Without truthfulness, progress and success in all of the worlds of God are impossible for a soul. When this holy attribute is established in man, all the divine qualities will also become realized." [10] Mere casual reflection tells us that if people were truthful in all their personal dealings and affairs, then misunderstanding, suspicion, hurt and anger would decrease, and trust, cooperation and service would increase. Truthfulness in the corporate and public world would be a great benefit to society, and would go a long way toward eliminating all those scandalous underhanded dealings that plague the business world today.

The collective form of truthfulness is consultation, the aim of which is to determine the truth in any matter by each one speaking truthfully his or her opinion on the matter at hand. Bahá'u'lláh admonishes: "Take ye counsel together in all matters, inasmuch as consultation is the lamp of guidance which leadeth the way, and is the bestower of understanding." (11) We'll return to consultation in the next question.

Third is trustworthiness. If we are lovingly caring for others, are cooperating with them, and are truthful in all matters, we are demonstrating trustworthiness, and that others may repose their trust in us to take care of the poor in our midst who are His trust. It is also trusting that we will be cared for in ways which we may not expect, know, or foresee.

So important is trustworthiness to human affairs that Bahá'u'lláh had a vision of trustworthiness as: "one of the Beauties of the Most Sublime Paradise, standing on a pillar of light, and calling aloud saying: "O inmates of earth and heaven! Behold ye My beauty, and My radiance, and My revelation, and My effulgence. By God, the True One! I am Trustworthiness and the revelation thereof, and the beauty thereof. I will recompense whosoever will cleave unto Me, and recognize My rank and station, and hold fast unto My hem. I am the most great ornament of the people of Baha, and the vesture of glory unto all who are in the kingdom of creation. I am the supreme instrument for the prosperity of the world, and the horizon of assurance unto all beings." Thus have We sent down for thee that which will draw men nigh unto the Lord of creation." (12) He also wrote: "O people! The goodliest vesture in the sight of God in this day is trustworthiness. All bounty and honour shall be the portion of the soul that arrayeth itself with this greatest of adornments." (13)

In yet another place He wrote: "We have enjoined upon all to become engaged in some trade or profession, and have accounted such occupation to be an act of worship. Before all else, however, thou shouldst receive, as a sign of God's acceptance, the mantle of trustworthiness from the hands of divine favour; for trustworthiness is the chief means of attracting confirmation and prosperity. We entreat God to make of it a radiant and mercifully showering rain-cloud that shall bring success and blessings to thy affairs. He of a truth is the All-Bountiful, the Gracious." [14]

"Commerce," He wrote in another connection, "is as a heaven, whose sun is trustworthiness and whose moon is truthfulness. The most precious of all things in the estimation of Him Who is the Sovereign Truth is trustworthiness: thus hath it been recorded in the sacred Scroll of God. Entreat ye the one true God to enable all mankind to attain to this most noble and lofty station." [15]

'Abdu'l-Baha said: "If a man were to perform every good work, yet fail in the least scruple to be entirely trustworthy and honest, his good works would become as dry tinder and his failure as a soul-consuming fire. If, on the other hand, he should fall short in all his affairs, yet act with trustworthiness and honesty, all his defects would ultimately be righted, all injuries remedied, and all infirmities healed. Our meaning is that, in the sight of God, trustworthiness is the bedrock of His Faith and the foundation of all virtues and perfections." [16]

Nothing more need be said about this virtue than what Bahá'u'lláh and 'Abdu'l-Baha wrote.

Fourth is faith: Faith is the greatest creative power within the human reality. It is an intrinsic impulse of the human spirit. 'Abdu'l-Bahá is reported to have said that: "nothing shall be impossible to you if you have faith….As ye have faith so shall your powers and blessings be." [17] Much of the hopelessness in today's world is really a lack of faith. But the lack of faith comes from the breakdown of trust, in oneself, in others and in institutions, because more and more relationships and arrangements don't work. Faith in relation to prosperity enables one to believe that: "The Spirit breathing through the Holy Scriptures is food for all who hunger. God Who has given the revelation to His Prophets will surely give of His abundance daily bread to all those who ask Him faithfully." [18]

We often say: "Seeing is believing." We mean by this little gnome of supposed insight that wisdom is to be skeptical of anything that can't be perceived with the naked eye. But actually the opposite is the truer account. Faith is neither blind belief, nor belief in something we cannot relate to. The Biblical statement of this attitude is Jesus' statement: "What things soever ye desire, when ye pray, believe that ye receive them, and ye shall have them" [19] Jesus is saying look into the world of vision, perceive with your spiritual eye, and believe that what you perceive there is real and can be manifested.

Many don't really believe what they mentally see, calling it "just imagination." This is doubt speaking through the poverty-mentality of the poor, puny-formed ego. Often such individuals lose heart and feel doubt when pursuing a dream, because they encounter obstacles or resistance. For them, this poverty thinking becomes a self-fulfilling belief: they are actually saying that they don't believe in the reality of spirit or that they are not deserving of something. Vision slides into dream which weakens into mere wish. Thus what they desire never manifests, and they rationalize with "It just didn't work out." But real faith enables one to persevere in the quest. Too, believing that one has received before he has actually received, as Jesus stated, means to make a place in one's life for the desired reality. If one is not prepared for the desired thing one is actually strengthening doubt not belief: doubt will increase and faith will decrease.

Fifth is generosity. Contrary to any Calvinist-type belief that accumulation of material riches is a sure sign of spiritual felicity, 'Abdu'l-Bahá says: "Eternal happiness is contingent upon giving." [20] There is no greater means to achieve general prosperity than via generosity. Bahá'u'lláh commands us: "Be ye the trustees of God amongst His creatures, and the emblems of His generosity amidst His people." (21) In another place He warns the wealthy, saying: "Tell the rich of the midnight sighing of the poor, lest heedlessness lead them into the path of destruction, and deprive them of the Tree of Wealth. To give and to be generous are attributes of Mine; well is it with him that adorneth himself with My virtues." (22) In a letter to the Central Organization for a Durable Peace, 'Abdu'l-Bahá wrote: "Among the teachings of Bahá'u'lláh is voluntary sharing of one's property with others among mankind. This voluntary sharing is greater than equality, and consists in this, that one should not prefer oneself to others, but rather should sacrifice one's life and property for others." (23) To the great financier and philanthropist, Andrew Carnegie, He wrote: "Man reacheth perfection through good deeds, voluntarily performed, not through good deeds the doing of which was forced upon him. And sharing is a personally chosen righteous act: that is, the rich should extend assistance to the poor, they should expend their substance for the poor, but of their own free will, and not because the poor have gained this end by force. For the harvest of force is turmoil and the ruin of the social order. On the other hand voluntary sharing, the freely-chosen expending of one's substance, leadeth to society's comfort and peace. It lighteth up the world; it bestoweth honour upon humankind." (24) While in Paris He said: "The rich must give of their abundance, they must soften their hearts and cultivate a compassionate intelligence, taking thought for those sad ones who are suffering from lack of the very necessities of life." (25)

But just to tell someone "be generous like Christ or Bahá'u'lláh" and quote a bunch of fine words probably will not get him or her very far. That is because to an immature soul, to give to another is to impoverish himself, for he thinks life is a competitive zero-sum game with only winners and losers. Spiritual giving is win/win. We are never in competition with each other when we are cooperating with higher powers. For in that cooperative relation there is plenty for all, and we need not fear running out of wealth, either personally or collectively. The spiritualized soul recognizes that the act of giving itself is wealth in a higher form and generates more of that wealth. This is our true affluence—a word which means "flows freely".

General prosperity is founded on and expressed through generosity. It is not those who have too little materially that are the truly poor. The truly poor are those who are poor in spirit.

Sixth is gratitude. Gratitude is an active power drawing to us the good pleasure of God—the first attracting the second. Gratitude works for prosperity by establishing good human relations and relations with divinity. Grace is the root of gratitude, so we should be grateful for our innate virtues and use them to contribute to prosperity.

'Abdul-Baha wrote: "There is a cordial thanksgiving, too, which expresses itself in the deeds and actions of man when his heart is filled with gratitude. For example, God has conferred upon man the gift of guidance, and in thankfulness for this great gift certain deeds must emanate from him. To express his gratitude for the favors of God man must show forth praiseworthy actions. In response to these bestowals he must render good deeds, be self-sacrificing, loving the servants of God, forfeiting even life for them, showing kindness to all the creatures." [26]

It takes but little effort to imagine other deeds and "praiseworthy actions" that would contribute to prosperity, besides the one's the Master lists: self-sacrificing, loving the servants of God, showing kindness to all creatures. The important point for this discussion is that we do these services for others to show our gratitude to God.

Seventh is humility. 'Abdu'l-Bahá was often likened to an ocean, not just because He seemed bigger than any situation, but also because His deep humility made Him put Himself lower than everyone else and thus willingly serve them. All waters flow to the ocean for it is at the lowest point, yet the ocean is also the fount of all life. So is service the fount of wealth. Humility is not such total self-effacement that one feels unworthy to do anything. Humility is an attitude that seeks out service; that always wishes to help. It should be a quality of the leaders of humankind.

Steven Covey, author of *Principle-Centered Leadership*, writes: "You can't have a oneness, a unity, without humility....The great servant leaders have that humility, the hallmark of inner religion." [27]

Eighth is detachment. Detachment is the opposite of attachment. It stems from having to steer through the push and pull of conflicting passions and positions. Detachment can only be maintained by being above opposition, by taking the wide and long view of things and events.

For wealth to circulate freely and **all** humanity made affluent, detachment from personal wealth is necessary. This attitude, in turn, arises from a consciousness of humanity's oneness. Baha'u'llah wrote: "Know ye not why We created you all from the same dust? That no one should exalt himself over the other. Ponder at all times in your hearts how ye were created. Since We have created you all from one same substance it is incumbent on you to be even as one soul, to walk with the same feet, eat with the same mouth and dwell in the same land, that from your inmost being, by your deeds and actions, the signs of oneness and the essence of detachment may be made manifest." [28] With detachment the fires of greed and avarice will be dampered, and the cold fears of insecurity dissolved.

Recall the discussion earlier about gold. Baha'u'llah stated: "Thou dost wish for gold and I desire thy freedom from it. Thou thinkest thyself rich in its possession, and I recognize thy wealth in thy sanctity therefrom." And: "Busy not thyself with this world, for with fire We test the gold, and with gold We test Our servants."

Though we are not to busy ourselves with this world, we also know that we are not to disengage from the problems and challenges facing humankind. We must do everything in our power to alleviate suffering and empower the disempowered. Baha'u'llah's counsel is: "Be anxiously concerned with the needs of the age ye live in, and center your deliberations on its exigencies and requirements." (29) Anxious concern cannot, in turn, harden into attachment to this or that outcome or result, nor can any attachment interfere with our purpose of attaining eternal life. Let us recall, regarding the Great Teachers, that: "The purpose underlying Their revelation hath been to educate all men, that they may, at the hour of death, ascend, in the utmost purity and sanctity and with absolute detachment, to the throne of the Most High." (30)

In the realm of action, detachment is to leave all things to God, the Universal Mind, to achieve any result wished for— so long as we are following and applying spiritual principle. But to be receptive to whatever God decides is not to forget about our desire and do nothing but listlessly wait for results to magically materialize. That would make apathy appear principled. We should let go of any notion of how we think the desire must be realized because the infinite Mind knows far better than we how to organize things to bring desired ends through the universal relationships organizing the world.

The essence of the virtue of detachment was summed up by Baha'u'llah in this way: "Should prosperity befall thee, rejoice not, and should abasement come upon thee, grieve not, for both shall pass away and be no more." (31) True detachment is from both prosperity and abasement. The reason for this is that fear and peril are imbedded in this world. We are in peril just by being in the world. Detachment is an ark.

Ninth is contentment. Contentment is the obverse of detachment and assists one to be detached. Baha'u'llah writes: "Put away all covetousness and seek contentment; for the covetous hath ever been deprived, and the contented hath ever been loved and praised." (32) The soul in the Valley of Contentment, Bahá'u'lláh says: "…feeleth the winds of divine contentment blowing from the plane of the spirit. He burneth away the veils of want, and with inward and outward eye, perceiveth within and without all things the day of: 'God will compensate each one out of His abundance.'" **(33)**

Contentment means to be satisfied with whatever God bestows. If we have the virtues of prosperity, practice them faithfully and with expectation and gratitude, and if still the desired reality does not manifest then it is for the best. Then contentment kicks in. All desires should be with the proviso: "If God so wishes." In this regard Bahá'u'lláh wrote to a petitioner: "Concerning thine own affairs, if thou wouldst content thyself with whatever might come to pass it would be praiseworthy. To engage in some profession is highly commendable, for when occupied with work one is less likely to dwell on the unpleasant aspects of life." **(34)** Truly contentment is a wonderful gem.

Tenth is Action in Service. Practice is the most important virtue. Action connects moral impulse with thought and deed to enable the current of spirit to flow into the world. Service is the currency of the moral economy. Services, not necessarily performed for pay, are new indicators of prosperity expressive of those riches we possess innately. Recall that spiritual transformation cannot occur absent the soul's "labor" to "translate that which hath been written into reality and action." Examining this key virtue in greater detail for education is the core of any answer to the final question: how to apply the knowledge gained from the first three questions.

****

These are my ten personal virtues of prosperity. These virtues transmute the base metal of ego thoughts and selfish actions into the pure gold of selfless moral behavior. They act to overcome and redirect a materialist value system revolving around me-first into a spiritual one based on you-before-me. These virtues oppose the lies, injustice, faithlessness, greed, irresponsibility, pride, discontent, and a passivity/predatory attitude characteristic of that me-first way of life. These virtues are some of the pillars of a proper spiritual education that when inculcated into the lives of individuals will "enable mankind to benefit therefrom." There is no doubt that if we nurture even some of them, new kinds of human interrelations will appear that shall create a new kind of civilization that embraces all in a world of peace and prosperity.

Again, knowledge of these virtues is not enough. They must be put into practice. But, except for the truly morally courageous, most people will consistently put them into practice only after being transformed by the Word of God. Why?

Consider: no one will deny that in a world where unconscionable amounts of poverty, inequity, exploitation, discrimination, and prejudice are allowed to exist, it is difficult to believe that just "being good" will do much good. The situation seems utterly hopeless to many, so they get what they can while they can. It seems human nature to do so. But that is because we are bucking hundreds of years of conditioning that has delayed our understanding of spiritual development, warped our thinking and blinded our insight, though we are, generally, unaware of this. It has also filled our minds with unmanageable levels of anxiety, fear, and insecurity, and we are acutely aware of this! From this perspective we can clearly note the deep understanding of human nature stated by the Universal House of Justice. They stated, remember, that once people "know the answers" to the first three questions "they need to be helped to gradually apply these answers to everyday behaviour." Applied spirituality is each individual's personal responsibility. But most of us must be assisted to apply this knowledge. Let us turn to the final question and discuss:

How to Apply the Knowledge?

Alas, notwithstanding the laudable efforts, in every land, of well-intentioned individuals working to improve circumstances in society, the obstacles preventing the realization of such vision seem insurmountable to many. Their hopes founder on erroneous assumptions about human nature that so permeate the structures and traditions of much of present-day living as to have attained the status of established fact. These assumptions appear to make no allowance for the extraordinary reservoir of spiritual potential available to any illumined soul who draws upon it; instead, they rely for justification on humanity's failings, examples of which daily reinforce a common sense of despair. A layered veil of false premises thus obscures a fundamental truth: The state of the world reflects a distortion of the human spirit, not its essential nature.
(The Universal House of Justice, Ridvan 2012)

Near the end of the Great Depression, in his inaugural address of January 20, 1937, President Franklin Roosevelt said: "We have always known that heedless self-interest was bad morals, now we know that it is bad economics."

I said at the beginning of this essay that to solve our economic crisis two kinds of education were required: spiritual or ideal, and material or practical. Of these two, the spiritual education was by far the more important one, so I have dwelt at some length upon it, as it not only renews a paradigm of economic thought and behavior, (i.e. the moral economy), but also implementing this paradigm ushers humanity out of its current economic malaise. But to answer the question of how to apply the knowledge of the answers to the first three questions, takes us to the practical side.

In practical education are learned the arts, sciences and skills needed for employment, the finding of one's calling, and personal arenas of service. Many educational systems today do an adequate job of preparing students for career, for employment, for going about the business of earning a living—that is, for entering the material economy—though in a world in fracture and disarray meeting those goals is increasingly problematical. But, without a consciousness of human oneness, conceptualizing the proper moral context for these remains an elusive goal. For, more than getting the skills needed to pursue such obvious material goals as a comfortable life, a practical education that prepares people to enter the moral economy must inculcate attitudes that empower the disempowered, that help generate sustainable material wealth by focusing upon stewardship of the renewable energy sources of sun, wind and water, and that remove all incentives to engage in war, exploitation and an unbridled profit-motive. Such education must also transform society at the levels of culture by training individuals in the arts of community-building and assisting them to practice the spiritual disciplines of meditation and consultation. Scattered through the essay in bits and pieces, much has already been said or implied on all this, because the central questions are not hermetically sealed from one another, but interact, mutually define, and cross-fertilize each other.

Regarding a proper education, which these last two paragraphs have helped to further delineate, the House of Justice wrote that youth must have a program that "engages their expanding consciousness in an exploration of reality that helps them to analyse the constructive and destructive forces operating in society and to recognize the influence these forces exert on their thoughts and actions, sharpening their spiritual perception, enhancing their powers of expression and reinforcing moral structures that will serve them throughout their lives. At an age when burgeoning intellectual, spiritual and physical powers become accessible to them, they are being given the tools needed to combat the forces that would rob them of their true identity as noble beings and to work for the common good." (1)

We are created rich in the spiritual wealth of virtue, but individuals need to know how to interpersonally bring these riches out of human nature and apply them in order to transform an increasingly dysfunctional materialist order into a functioning spiritual one. Materialism is really the legitimate desire for prosperity gone hideously awry, and the creators of this illusion are transfixed by their own creation. Two of the most powerful and underutilized methods of investigating reality and dispelling illusion are meditation and consultation.

Meditation has recently been explored scientifically as the profound learning tool that it really is So important is meditation that the Master tells us: 'You cannot apply the name 'man' to any being void of the faculty of meditation, without it he would be a mere animal, lower than the beasts. Through the faculty of meditation man attains to eternal life; through it he receives the breath of the Holy Spirit." (2)

Meditation brings forth knowledge that is, in some sense, already within the soul. For example, 'Abdu'l-Bahá remarks: "It is an axiomatic fact that while you meditate you are speaking with your own spirit. In that state of mind you put certain questions to your spirit and the spirit answers: the light breaks forth and the reality is revealed....the bestowal of the Spirit is given in reflection and meditation. The spirit of man is itself informed and strengthened during meditation, through it affairs of which man knew nothing are unfolded to his view....Meditation is the key for opening the doors of mysteries. In that state man abstracts himself, in that subjective mood he is immersed in the ocean of spiritual life and can unfold the secrets of things-in-themselves....the faculty of meditation frees man from his animal nature, discerns the reality of things, puts man in touch with God. This faculty brings forth from the invisible plane the sciences and arts." **(3)** In other words, meditation and reflection as modes of knowing are the means of acquiring conscious knowledge of and from the spirit, a genuine gnosis, an experiential not intellectual knowledge not of God directly but of "My light within thee." **(4)** And this light can illumine any problem and challenge.

Another practice by which understanding functions is consultation. While meditation is an individual investigation of reality, consultation is, primarily, the collective investigation of reality. Baha'u'llah declares: "Consultation bestoweth greater awareness and transmuteth conjecture into certitude. It is a shining light which, in a dark world, leadeth the way and guideth. For everything there is and will continue to be a station of perfection and maturity. The maturity of the gift of understanding is made manifest through consultation." **(5)** He also stated: "Take ye counsel together in all matters, inasmuch as consultation is the lamp of guidance which leadeth the way, and is the bestower of understanding." **(6)**

Through consultation that employs the best of current scientific understanding and technology, the knowledge gained from answering the three previous questions can be applied. When such consultation is guided by spiritual principles the higher self within us is aroused, its powers and capacities are released, and the correct moral perspective comprehended. Spiritual principles reconnect the soul with its sacred Root, restoring that of which improper education has deprived us. Ideally, spiritual principle, scientific knowledge, technology, and practical action should be one seamless and mutually reinforcing flow of thought and behavior, the means to achieve coherence between the spiritual and the material. We do not live in such an ideal condition, of course, rather one almost exactly the opposite of it. Much needs to change in society.

Hence, students must also be taught the skills of critical thinking and evaluation in order to comprehensively analyze their social and intellectual environment in the light of spiritual principles and material forces to understand their interplay, to decide if these forces are weaving the threads of a sustainable social system, and, if not, decide upon the means to bring about a positive change, execute a plan of action, reflect upon the outcome and start the cycle of learning again. One investigates reality to learn to weed out erroneous beliefs and practices and replace them with better ones. This does not go on without some pushback from the entrenched order.

I mean that one thing should be clear: applying spiritual principles of thought and behavior among people whose values are materialistic, whose conception of human nature is ego-centered, and whose idea of human purpose is self-centered action, creates upheaval, arouses suspicion, and invites negative reaction. Baha'u'llah wrote of the effects of individual virtuous acts: "One righteous act is endowed with a potency that can so elevate the dust as to cause it to pass beyond the heaven of heavens. It can tear every bond asunder, and hath the power to restore the force that hath spent itself and vanished." [7] I call your attention to the "tear every bond asunder" effect sandwiched between the two sparkling promises.

At the interpersonal level, there is no way to change society other than practice, practice, practice. Recall the Universal House of Justice's statement on influencing economic life: "The light of the Revelation is destined to illumine every sphere of endeavor; in each, the relationships that sustain society are to be recast; in each, the world seeks examples of how human beings should be to one another. We offer for your consideration, given its conspicuous part in generating the ferment in which so many people have recently been embroiled, the economic life of humanity, where injustice is tolerated with indifference and disproportionate gain is regarded as the emblem of success. So deeply entrenched are such pernicious attitudes that it is hard to imagine how any one individual can alone alter the prevailing standards by which the relationships in this domain are governed. Nevertheless, there are certain practices a Bahá'í would eschew, such as dishonesty in one's transactions or the economic exploitation of others. Faithful adherence to the divine admonitions demands there be no contradiction between one's economic conduct and one's beliefs as a Baha'i. By applying in one's life those principles of the Faith that relate to fairness and equity, a single soul can uphold a standard far above the low threshold by which the world measures itself. Humanity is weary for want of a pattern of life to which to aspire." **(8)**

Bahá'u'lláh outlined a pattern of life to which every individual can aspire: "Be generous in prosperity, and thankful in adversity. Be worthy of the trust of thy neighbor, and look upon him with a bright and friendly face. Be a treasure to the poor, an admonisher to the rich, an answerer of the cry of the needy, a preserver of the sanctity of thy pledge. Be fair in thy judgment, and guarded in thy speech. Be unjust to no man, and show all meekness to all men. Be as a lamp unto them that walk in darkness, a joy to the sorrowful, a sea for the thirsty, a haven for the distressed, an upholder and defender of the victim of oppression. Let integrity and uprightness distinguish all thine acts. Be a home for the stranger, a balm to the suffering, a tower of strength for the fugitive. Be eyes to the blind, and a guiding light unto the feet of the erring. Be an ornament to the countenance of truth, a crown to the brow of fidelity, a pillar of the temple of righteousness, a breath of life to the body of mankind, an ensign of the hosts of justice, a luminary above the horizon of virtue, a dew to the soil of the human heart, an ark on the ocean of knowledge, a sun in the heaven of bounty, a gem on the diadem of wisdom, a shining light in the firmament of thy generation, a fruit upon the tree of humility." **(9)**

These admonitions, while pointing to an upsetting of the established "moral" applecart, also point to the need to reset human society upon a new moral foundation. To recast the personal relationships that sustain society is to recast society from the ground up. As more individuals enter the moral economy of sharing, service and self-sacrifice, which is the exchange of spirit and true humanity, that economy gathers volume and momentum. The moral potentialialities within more human hearts are mysteriously activated. Every act of service creates more spiritual riches. This spiritual energy cascades upwards and outward in warming currents of virtue to find form in new civic relations which are the foundation for cultural expressions which blossom into coordinating political arrangements which can organize a global commonwealth of peace and prosperity.

By now it should be obvious that the inherently divisive and obsessively polarizing ego-based values and actions that have informed human relations for centuries are not the source of attitudes of cooperation, altruism, sharing and giving that are the basis of human prosperity, but are the very antithesis of them. There is no doubt that spiritual behavior cannot appear so long as we remain at the level of ego-consciousness, however idealistic it can appear to be. Trying to creating unity and prosperity from a nature that knows only disunity and poverty sets one up for failure, for the harder one tries the farther one gets from the goal. True prosperity can only be founded upon a consciousness of humanity's oneness. Spiritually-inspired action can only come out of this consciousness, which is educed by spiritual principles and virtuous acts. This is the prerequisite for all other activity. But also criteria that measure the wealth of the moral economy are needed. [10]

The Poor are First

In the dominant material economy wealth is measured in financial terms, by the number and quality of goods available, the capital needed to produce these goods and deliver them to consumers, and the amount of money one has to purchase these commodities, whether goods or services, materials or peoples. There are also service indicators to measure the social wealth of a society, such as literacy rates, health care delivery, numbers of children in school, and the like. This wealth is aggregated under names such as Gross Domestic Product which are put forth as a supposed measure of how rich the whole society is: nevermind that the majority of people may be living under the poverty line—another abstract category of numbers—and be unable to take advantage of services supposedly available to them.

In short, in the material economy wealth is measured by the wealth of the wealthy, both personally and corporately. And, if the rich are richer, then everyone must be richer, right? Wrong! This "bad economics", as Roosevelt called it, has lead to the situation described by 'Abdu'l-Baha: "We see amongst us men who are overburdened with riches on the one hand, and on the other those unfortunate ones who starve with nothing; those who possess several stately palaces, and those who have not where to lay their head. Some we find with numerous courses of costly and dainty food; whilst others can scarce find sufficient crusts to keep them alive. Whilst some are clothed in velvets, furs and fine linen, others have insufficient, poor and thin garments with which to protect them from the cold. This condition of affairs is wrong, and must be remedied."

His remedy on the institutional and governmental level is based on the following principle: "One of the most important principles of the Teaching of Bahá'u'lláh is: The right of every human being to the daily bread whereby they exist, or the equalization of the means of livelihood.

"The arrangements of the circumstances of the people must be such that poverty shall disappear, that everyone, as far as possible, according to his rank and position, shall share in comfort and well-being....There must be special laws made, dealing with these extremes of riches and of want. The members of the Government should consider the laws of God when they are framing plans for the ruling of the people. The general rights of mankind must be guarded and preserved.

"The government of the countries should conform to the Divine Law which gives equal justice to all. This is the only way in which the deplorable superfluity of great wealth and miserable, demoralizing, degrading poverty can be abolished. Not until this is done will the Law of God be obeyed." [11]

In the moral economy wealth can be measured by the services and self-sacrifices community members render each other, especially to the poor, dispossessed, and unfortunate. The number of services performed for others or the common good is an indicator of the spiritual wealth of society. That is, in the moral economy, the poor are not a problem, but, paradoxically, the solution to spiritual poverty; not the challenge but the opportunity for spiritual growth: better morals not more money is the primary answer. It is the poverty-mentality and its associated attitudes of greed, self-interest, and entitlement that are the problem and the challenge. The yardstick which measures spiritual wealth is not numbers—after all, designated enumerators can't wander around adding up the number of good deeds reportedly performed daily. Rather, increased spiritual wealth is measured by a heightened sense of well-being and security, of being loved and loving; by the willingness to be kind and to sacrifice for one's neighbor, conditions which are felt among the members of a community. Spiritual acts may be hidden, but their effects cannot be. However subjective these measures may be at present, they are real and can achieve conscious expression, notation and quiet influence. The ten virtues of prosperity could serve as indicators of a community's spiritual capital being invested in and for the common good.

Baha'u'llah admonishes: "Man's merit lieth in service and virtue and not in the pageantry of wealth and riches....Dissipate not the wealth of your precious lives in the pursuit of evil and corrupt affection, nor let your endeavors be spent in promoting your personal interest." [12] 'Abdu'l-Baha echoes this sentiment: "the happiness and greatness, the rank and station, the pleasure and peace, of an individual have never consisted in his personal wealth, but rather in his excellent character, his high resolve, the breadth of his learning, and his ability to solve difficult problems." [13]

As I have stated, in the moral economy material wealth must of course be generated. But we are not after material wealth per se. We are after prosperity. Wealth is absolutely essential for prosperity to mean anything, but wealth itself is not prosperity. Prosperity is the combining of spiritual riches with material wealth. Wealth can be used to build hospitals or bombs. But prosperity makes one decision infinitely better than the other, and that decision is the province of the moral economy. Either way, wealth is like having a hammer to drive a nail. Poverty is like having only your hand to do it.

Prosperity is achieved through a change from me-first to you-before-me, from looking out for number one to caring for each other, especially those most in need. 'Abdu'l-Bahá says: "Think ye at all times of rendering some service to every member of the human race. Pay ye no heed to aversion and rejection, to disdain, hostility, injustice: act ye in the opposite way. Be ye sincerely kind, not in appearance only. Let each one of God's loved ones centre his attention on this: to be the Lord's mercy to man; to be the Lord's grace. Let him do some good to every person whose path he crosseth, and be of some benefit to him. Let him improve the character of each and all, and reorient the minds of men."[14] Bahá'u'lláh warns succinctly: "Beware lest ye prefer yourselves above your neighbors."[15]

While the actual wealth in circulation of the moral economy is the services performed, the untapped potential wealth in a moral economy is the poor, who are the trust of God. That is, our untapped wealth is not just in earthly mines, but in the mines rich in gems called human souls. Why? In fixing society's unjust relations with its poor—i.e. the inequities of opportunity in education, jobs, taxes, and the like—resides the unmined wealth of services that will increase the spiritual and material capital of everyone. 'Abdu'l-Baha stated: "What could be better before God than thinking of the poor? For the poor are beloved by our heavenly Father. When Christ came upon the earth, those who believed in Him and followed Him were the poor and lowly, showing that the poor were near to God. When a rich man believes and follows the Manifestation of God, it is a proof that his wealth is not an obstacle and does not prevent him from attaining the pathway of salvation. After he has been tested and tried, it will be seen whether his possessions are a hindrance in his religious life. But the poor are especially beloved of God.

Their lives are full of difficulties, their trials continual, their hopes are in God alone. Therefore, you must assist the poor as much as possible, even by sacrifice of yourself. No deed of man is greater before God than helping the poor. Spiritual conditions are not dependent upon the possession of worldly treasures or the absence of them." [16]

It is moral wealth when the rich serve the poor, whose care is entrusted to them by God, by voluntary sharing of their wealth to alleviate whatever sufferings they can. But, more importantly, the rich can contribute to the common good by empowering the poor through such actions as promoting education, encouraging industry, and offering skills training. Such service also expands the material economy by increasing the number of its skilled workers. To recall a previous quote from 'Abdu'l-Baha: "Wealth is most commendable, provided the entire population is wealthy. If, however, a few have inordinate riches while the rest are impoverished, and no fruit or benefit accrues from that wealth, then it is only a liability to its possessor. If, on the other hand, it is expended for the promotion of knowledge, the founding of elementary and other schools, the encouragement of art and industry, the training of orphans and the poor—in brief, if it is dedicated to the welfare of society—its possessor will stand out before God and man as the most excellent of all who live on earth and will be accounted as one of the people of paradise." [17]

These are acts of social justice, and "the best beloved of all things in My sight is Justice."[18] In this same regard Baha'u'llah warns: "Know ye that the poor are the trust of God in your midst. Watch that ye betray not His trust, that ye deal not unjustly with them and that ye walk not in the ways of the treacherous. Ye will most certainly be called upon to answer for His trust on the day when the Balance of Justice shall be set, the day when unto everyone shall be rendered his due, when the doings of all men, be they rich or poor, shall be weighed." [19]

It is also moral wealth for the poor to strive to earn their livelihood, so that they may contribute to the production side of the material economy. By becoming materially better off they, too, add to the moral economy because, as 'Abdu'l-Baha indicated, provided people act moderately, wealth augments spirituality. The poor must become wealthier so that they may add their full share to the common wealth and to general prosperity. In these complementary acts of service to the common weal the prosperity of society will increase.

Knowing this much is not much. Action must follow principle. The Master said: "Knowledge is not enough; we hope by the Love of God we shall put it into practice. A spiritual universal Force is needed for this. Meetings are good for engendering spiritual force. To know that it is possible to reach a state of perfection, is good; to march forward on the path is better. We know that to help the poor and to be merciful is good and pleases God, but knowledge alone does not feed the starving man, nor can the poor be warmed by knowledge or words in the bitter winter; we must give the practical help of Loving-kindness." [20]

Giving for the good of our fellow man, undeterred by the fear of poverty, is the fundamental individual act of social and economic justice. By giving directly of their wealth to the needy or to charitable and philanthropic agencies, the fortunate aid those they may neither know nor encounter, and who can not necessarily benefit them in return. We may think that human nature being what it is, such thoughts while nice are not "realistic", or are spasmodic at best, and that is the best that can be hoped for. However accurate that assessment may be in one's personal experience, such pessimism stems from a wrong view of human nature, which comes from an improper education. "Qualities of spirit and heart are extremely contagious", said the Master. Let us test that statement in our daily lives. We can not wait for the other person to be the first to sacrifice, or for another to put us before him. Every individual must follow the lead of the world's great Luminaries, for those who are not busy changing the world are busy keeping it the way it is—and the way the world is, is terribly wrong.

Final Thoughts

I created thee rich, why dost thou bring thyself down to poverty?
(Baha'u'llah, *The Hidden Words* #13 Arabic)

    This essay has provided one possible answer to Baha'u'llah's question above, namely, we are victims of an improper education that deprives us of that which we inherently possess. Such education denies that we are created rich in powerful virtues and instead brings perception and self-knowledge down to a poverty of self-interested ego impulses.

    Knowing one is created rich gives one the freedom and resources to determine, so far as determination, initiative and thought can do, one's life and destiny. Further, if every individual is rich, then the collective, humanity, must be innately a colossus of wealth. Bringing ourselves down to poverty is to strap our souls to the grind of grim material necessity, that endlessly revolving gerbil wheel of natural causation and cycles which are impersonal and seem irresistible and beyond our control. It is to live in a de-humanized state of nature, existing in a condition of perpetual want and misery, enslaved to biological and psychological needs, to be bottle-fed on anxiety and nursed by fear, captive to the urgencies of physical life and ferociously competitive about getting them.

    Rather, every individual is a mine created rich in gems of spiritual virtue; a miraculous talisman that can attract divinity and all created things to it, including wealth, because the riches of the universe are enfolded within it; a being of thought and will with aptitudes and innate gifts, and, once mature, the willingness and desire to use wealth wisely by contributing to the common wealth. These are essential to knowing one's self.

True prosperity is where the spiritual and the material are in harmonious balance for everyone, not just for oneself. Humanity is, generally speaking, far too concerned with its material side and is locked in a poverty mentality. The solution to the economic problem is fundamentally a spiritual one, because the "problem" is a lack of spiritual development. Spiritual resources are in abundance for we are created rich. Spiritually, wealth is not something we need but something we are. More spirit, not just more goods, is the answer, and infusing more spirit into society means, illogically to the poverty-mind, sharing generously. In sharing, material security will be achieved for all. So a spiritual solution to the economic problem means, for me, to use our inner spiritual resources to create this balance, to mine and express those inner gems deposited within the soul of every human being in order to bring about the death of scarcity. I truly believe that spiritual education can accomplish this.

Now is the time to do this. Humanity has reached maturity.[1] Wealth is needed, for the purpose of wealth is to augment spirituality. We already quoted 'Abdu'l-Bahá on this, but it is worth repeating His words: "Provided they behave moderately, the more people advance in the material realm, the more their capacity for spirituality is augmented."

From all that has been said and quoted: "it is clear that the honor and exaltation of man must be something more than material riches. Material comforts are only a branch, but the root of the exaltation of man is the good attributes and virtues which are the adornments of his reality. These are the divine appearances, the heavenly bounties, the sublime emotions, the love and knowledge of God; universal wisdom, intellectual perception, scientific discoveries, justice, equity, truthfulness, benevolence, natural courage and innate fortitude; the respect for rights and the keeping of agreements and covenants; rectitude in all circumstances; serving the truth under all conditions; the sacrifice of one's life for the good of all people; kindness and esteem for all nations; obedience to the teachings of God; service in the Divine Kingdom; the guidance of the people, and the education of the nations and races. This is the prosperity of the human world! This is the exaltation of man in the world! This is eternal life and heavenly honor!

"These virtues do not appear from the reality of man except through the power of God and the divine teachings, for they need supernatural power for their manifestation. It may be that in the world of nature a trace of these perfections may appear, but they are unstable and ephemeral; they are like the rays of the sun upon the wall." [2] But we must first have the resolve to swim against the tide. That is easier when we swim together and accompany each other on the journey.

I will close this essay with two statements, the first a warning, the second a promise. The Universal House of justice warned that "true prosperity, the fruit of a dynamic coherence between the material and spiritual requirements of life, will recede further and further out of reach as long as consumerism continues to act as opium to the human soul." [3] Thus in a stunning reversal of a famous phrase, not religion, but, rather, materialism and its rotten fruit, consumerism, is the true opiate of the people.

The promise is part of a statement addressed by 'Abdu'l-Baha to the readers of The Christian Commonwealth, 1 January 1913: "The Lord of all mankind hath fashioned this human realm to be a Garden of Eden, an earthly paradise. If, as it must, it findeth the way to harmony and peace, to love and mutual trust, it will become a true abode of bliss, a place of manifold blessings and unending delights. Therein shall be revealed the excellence of humankind, therein shall the rays of the Sun of Truth shine forth on every hand." [4] Let us arise and shake off the spiritual torpor that has fallen upon the soul and energetically find our way to harmony and peace, to love and mutual trust, and together re-enter the Garden.

Notes

Introduction

1. Baha'u'llah's full statement is: "Man is the supreme Talisman. Lack of a proper education hath, however, deprived him of that which he doth inherently possess." (*Tablets of Baha'u'llah*: 161.

2. The Holy Bible, *The Book of Proverbs* 29:18

3. The Universal House of Justice, message dated July 21, 1968 to a National Spiritual Assembly.

4. Mircea Eliade, *The Sacred and the Profane*: 126.

5. King James Bible, The Book of Matthew 16:25. No better restatement of Christ's words can be found than in the recent apostolic exhortation of Pope Francis titled Joy of the Gospel. Just beautiful! He wrote: "As long as the problems of the poor are not radically resolved by rejecting the absolute autonomy of markets and financial speculation and by attacking the structural causes of inequality, no solution will be found for the world's problems or, for that matter, to any problems."

6. The term "social code" is from Shoghi Effendi. "Does not the very operation of the world-unifying forces that are at work in this age necessitate that He Who is the Bearer of the Message of God in this day should not only reaffirm that self-same exalted standard of individual conduct inculcated by the Prophets gone before Him, but embody in His appeal, to all governments and peoples, the essentials of that social code, that Divine Economy, which must guide humanity's concerted efforts in establishing that all-embracing federation which is to

signalize the advent of the Kingdom of God on this earth?" (*The World Order of Baha'u'llah*: 60)

7. A good deal of exposition has, of course, already been done, going back as far as Baha'u'llah Himself. Recently there are the following brilliant statements from the Baha'i International Community: 1993 Apr 01, *Sustainable Development and the Human Spirit;* March 1995, *The Prosperity of Humankind*; October 1995 *Turning Point For All Nations*; March 1996, *United Nations Decade for Human Rights Education*; 1998 *Valuing Spirituality in Development*; 3 May 2010, *Rethinking Prosperity: Forging Alternatives to a Culture of Consumerism*. Also: *A Bahá'í Perspective on Economics of the Future*. Compiled by Badi Shams. New Delhi: Bahá'í Publishing Trust. 2009 reprint.

8. 'Abdu'l-Baha often referred to humanity through the metaphor of the household. For example: "Although the body politic is one family yet because of lack of harmonious relations some members are comfortable and some in direst misery, some members are satisfied and some are hungry, some members are clothed in most costly garments and some families are in need of food and shelter. Why? Because this family lacks the necessary reciprocity and symmetry. This household is not well arranged. This household is not living under a perfect law." (*Foundations of World Unity*:38) Or: "As this human world is one household, why should its members be occupied with animosity and contention?" (*The Promulgation of Universal Peace*: 107)

9. Barnes, William. *Renewing the Sacred*. Self-published through Createspace. 2012.

10. Universal House of Justice, *The Promise World Peace*: 3.

11. Nowak, Martin A. and Highfield, Roger. *Super Cooperators: Altruism, Evolution, and Why We Need each Other to Succeed.* New York: Free Press. 2012.

12. Axelrod, Robert. *The Evolution of Cooperation.* Revised Edition. New York: Basic Books. 2006.

13. *Higher Social Class Predicts Increased Unethical Behavior* 27 February 2012, Proceedings of the National Academy of Sciences, Paul K. Piff, Daniel M. Stancato, Stéphane Côté, Rodolfo Mendoza-Denton, Dacher Keltner. Exploring the same terrain but on the macro-sociological level is Tyler, George R. *What Went Wrong: How the 1% Hijacked the American Middle Class . . . and What Other Countries Got Right.* Dallas: BenBella Books 2013.

Wisdom and Wealth: The Catalyst of Transformation

1. This is true even at the global level, for the world's circulation of wealth must keep pace with demand for it. There are two main problems at the global financial level. Accumulating countries such as China and Saudi Arabia are in conflict with spending countries like the United States, Japan and the wealthier countries of Europe. If too much of the world's wealth winds up in too few places the world system grinds to a halt. If it is spent too fast the system overheats and there is runaway inflation. This is outwardly a problem of different national levels of social and material development, and different stages of industrial life. But even here at the relations of nations I believe that problems can only be solved through a conscious application of spiritual principles growing out of a consciousness of humanity's oneness.

2. The Universal House of Justice, *Messages from the Universal House of Justice 1963-1986*: 283.

3. Baha'u'llah, *Gleanings from the Writings of Baha'u'llah*: 216.

4. The Universal House of Justice, 2002 April, *To the World's Religious Leaders*, p. 4.

5. Shoghi Effendi, *Principles of Bahá'í Administration*: 95.

6. Baha'u'llah, *The Hidden Words* #53Persian.

7. 'Abdu'l-Baha. *The Secret of Divine Civilization*: 24.

8. *Baha'i Prayers*: 161.

9. Abdu'l-Baha, *The Promulgation of Universal Peace*: 131.

10. *The Promulgation of Universal Peace*: 329.

11. Baha'i International Community, 1996 Mar 15, United Nations Decade for Human Rights Education.

12. Baha'u'llah, *Tablets of Baha'u'llah*: 87.

Who are you?

1. 'Abdu'l-Baha, *Some Answered Questions*: 212.

2. 'Abdu'l-Baha, *Selections from the Writings of 'Abdu'l-Bahá*: 139.

3. *Some Answered Questions*: 8

4. *The Promulgation of Universal Peace*: 329-330.

5. 'Abdu'l-Baha, *Paris Talks*: 60.

6. '*Some Answered Questions*: 235.

7. *Selections from the Writings of Abdu'l-Baha*: 130.

8. '*Some Answered Questions*: 235

9. From a letter written on behalf of Shoghi Effendi to Alfred Lunt, 1936. (*Lights of Guidance*: 208.)

10. *Selections from the Writings of Abdu'l-Baha*: 76.

11. Universal House of Justice, *Messages 1963 to 1986*: 376

12. *Some Answered Questions*: 236

13. Ibid.: 215.

14. *Paris Talks*: 107.

15. 'Abdu'l-Baha, Shoghi Effendi, *Japan Will Turn Ablaze*: 42.

16. Baha'u'llah, *Tablets of Baha'u'llah*: 161.

17. Baha'u'llah, *The Hidden Words*, Arabic #13.

18. The Holy Bible, *The Book of Genesis* 1:26.

19. *Tablets of Bahá'u'lláh*:163.

20. *Tablets of Baha'u'llah*:138.

21. *The Promulgation of Universal Peace*: 51.

22. Baha'i International Community, 1992 May 29, *Statement on Baha'u'llah*: 10.

23. Baha'u'llah. *The Seven Valleys and The Four Valleys*: 34.

24. *The Hidden Words*, Arabic #13.

25. Baha'u'llah. *The Seven Valleys and The Four Valleys*: 63.

26. 'Abdu'l-Baha, *Some Answered Questions*: 79-80.

27. *Gleanings from the Writings of Baha'u'llah*: 134.

28. Baha'u'llah, *Prayers and Meditations by Baha'u'llah*: 250.

29. Ibid. 314.

30. *The Promulgation of Universal Peace*: 329.

31. Baha'i International Community, 1998 Feb 18, *Valuing Spirituality in Development*.

32. Baha'u'llah, *Tablets of Baha'u'llah*: 52.

33. Baha'i International Community, 1995, March 03, *The Prosperity of Humankind*: 3.

34. *Tablets of Baha'u'llah*: 164.

35. From a letter of the Universal House of Justice to the Bahá'í youth of the world, January 1984.

36. *Paris Talks*: 90

37. *Gleanings from the Writings of Baha'u'llah*: 200.

38. *Paris Talks:* 21.

39. *Selections from the Writings of Abdu'l-Baha*: 136.

40. Baha'u'llah, *The Book of Certitude*: 240-1.

41. *Gleanings from the Writings of Baha'u'llah*: 149.

To what purpose do we exist?

1. Shoghi Effendi, *Directives from the Guardian*: 86.

2. *Gleanings from the Writings of Bahá'u'lláh*: 328-329.

3. *Selections from the Writings of 'Abdu'l-Bahá*: 177.

4. *Tablets of Baha'u'llah:* 219.

5. Ibid. 219.

6. Shoghi Effendi, *Directives from the Guardian*: 86.

7. *Paris Talks:* 17.

8. *The Hidden Words* #56 Arabic.

9. *The Hidden Words* #55 Arabic.

10. *Gleanings from the Writings of Baha'u'llah*: 276.

11. *The Hidden Words* #53 Arabic.

12. *The Hidden Words* #51 Persian.

13. *Ibid.*

14. Baha'u'llah, The *Summons of the Lord of Hosts*: 87.

15. *Gleanings from the Writings of Bahá'u'lláh*: 156-157.

16. *The Promulgation of Universal Peace*: 33.

17. 'Abdu'l-Baha, *The Secret of Divine Civilization*: 46.

18. *Tablets of Baha'u'llah*: 166.

19. *Gleanings from the Writings of Bahá'u'lláh*: 287.

20. *Gleanings from the Writings of Bahá'u'lláh*: 196.

21. *Gleanings from the Writings of Bahá'u'lláh*: 8.

22. *Tablets of Baha'u'llah*: 144.

23. King James Bible, The Book of Romans 12:6.

24. *Gleanings from the Writings of Bahá'u'lláh*: 202.

25. *Gleanings from the Writings of Bahá'u'lláh*: 215.

26. The Universal House of Justice Ridvan 2012.

27. Two excellent works examining the spiritual enterprise are: Lawrence Miller, *Spiritual Enterprise: Building Your Business in the Spirit of Service*. Oxford: George Ronald. 2007, and Don Brown, *To Build Anew: Creating Baha'i-inspired Enterprises*. British Columbia: Paragon-Quest Publications. 2002.

28. *Gleanings from the Writings of Bahá'u'lláh*: 287.

29. Baha'i International Community, 1995 Oct, *Turning Point For All Nations*.

30. *The Hidden Words* #80 Persian.

31. *Tablets of Bahá'u'lláh:* 267.

32. *Tablets of Baha'u'llah*: 26.

33. Baha'i International Community, 1995 Mar 03, *The Prosperity of Humankind*

34. From a letter written on behalf of Shoghi Effendi to the National Spiritual Assembly of the United States and Canada, March 22, 1937. (Compilations, *Lights of Guidance*: 623)

35. *Tablets of Baha'u'llah*: 26.

36. *Paris Talks*:176)

37. *Tablets of Baha'u'llah*: 26.

38. From a letter written on behalf of Shoghi Effendi to the National Spiritual Assembly of the United States and Canada, March 22, 1937. (Compilations, *Lights of Guidance*: 623)

39. *Tablets of Baha'u'llah*: 38

40. *Tablets of Baha'u'llah*: 51.

41. The Compilation of Compilations vol. I, p. 3.

42. *The Hidden Words* #82 Persian.

43. *Tablets of Baha'u'llah*: 155.

44. *Paris Talks*: 109.

45. *The Secret of Divine Civilization*: 24-25.

46. *Tablets of Baha'u'llah*: 34.

47. Compilations, *Lights of Guidance*: 210.

48. *Mahmud's Diary*: 122.

49. *Promulgation of Universal Peace*: 216

50. *Tablets of Baha'u'llah*: 71.

51. *Gleanings from the Writings of Bahá'u'lláh*: 202.

52. *Paris Talks*: 63.

53. *Tablets of Baha'u'llah*: 57.

54. Baha'i International Community, 1998 Feb 18, *Valuing Spirituality in Development*.

55. *Tablets of Baha'u'llah*: 71.

56. *Gleanings from the Writings of Bahá'u'lláh*: 278.

57. Baha'u'llah, *Epistle to the Son of the Wolf*: 54-55.

How should we act towards one another?

1. *Selections from the Writings of 'Abdu'l-Bahá*: 103.

2. *Gleanings from the Writings of Bahá'u'lláh*: 9

3. *Tablets of Baha'u'llah*: 86

4. *Gleanings from the Writings of Bahá'u'lláh*: 323.

5. *Selections from the Writings of 'Abdu'l-Bahá*: 206.

6. *Some Answered Questions*: 214. A recent study conducted by UC Berkeley and UC San Diego researchers and reported in the Huffington Post, November 27, 2013, found that generosity and

goodwill are infectious. The article states: "The findings suggest consumers' senses of fairness and reciprocity may be just as strong or stronger of a driving force in purchasing decisions than the desire to score the best deal."

7. *The Promulgation of Universal Peace*: 238-239.

8. *The Seven Valleys and the Four Valleys*: 58.

9. *Selections from the Writings of Abdu'l-Baha*: 27.

10. Cited by Shoghi Effendi in *The Advent of Divine Justice*: 21.

11. *Tablets of Baha'u'llah*: 168.

12. *Tablets of Bahá'u'lláh*: 37-38.

13. *The Compilation of Compilations* vol. II: 327.

14. *The Compilation of Compilations* vol. II: 335.

15. *The Compilation of Compilations* vol. II: 335-336.

16. *The Compilation of Compilations* vol. II: 339-340.

17. *Bahiyyih Khanum*: 225.

18. *Paris Talks:* 57.

19. The Holy Bible, *The Book of Mark* 11:24.

20. *The Promulgation of Universal Peace*: 131.

21. *Gleanings from the Writings of Bahá'u'lláh*: 297.

22. *The Hidden Words* #49 Persian.

23. *Selections from the Writings of Abdu'l-Baha*: 302.

24. *Ibid*: 114.

25. *Paris Talks:* 153

26. *The Promulgation of Universal Peace*: 236.

27. Steven R. Covey, *Principle-Centered Leadership*: 92.

28. *The Hidden Words* #68 Arabic.

29. *Gleanings from the Writings of* Baha'u'llah: 213.

30. *Gleanings from the Writings of Baha'u'llah*: 156-157.

31. *The Hidden Words* #52 Arabic.

32. *The Hidden Words* #50 Persian.

33. *The Seven Valleys and the Four Valleys*: 29.

34. *Tablets of Bahá'u'lláh*: 175.

How to Apply the Knowledge

1. The Universal House of Justice Ridvan 2010.

2. *Paris Talks*: 174.

3. Ibid. 174.

4. *The Hidden Words* #11 Arabic.

5. *The Compilation of Compilations* vol. I: 93.

6. *Tablets of Baha'u'llah*: 168.

7. *Gleanings from the Writings of Baha'u'llah*: 287.

8. The Universal House of Justice Ridvan 2012.

9. *Gleanings from the Writings of Baha'u'llah*: 284.

10. See, for example, the statement by the Bahá'í International Community, *Valuing Spirituality in Development: Initial Considerations Regarding the Creation of Spiritually Based Indicators for Development.*

11. *Paris* Talks: 151-154

12. *Tablets of Baha'u'llah*: 138.

13. *The Secret of Divine Civilization*: 23.

14. *Selections from the Writings of Abdu'l-Baha*: 3.

15. *Gleanings from the Writings of Baha'u'llah*: 315.

16. *Promulgation of Universal Peace,* 216.

17. *The Secret of Divine Civilization*: 23.

18. *The Arabic Hidden Words #2.*

19. *Gleanings from the Writings of Baha'u'llah*: 251

20. Abdu'l-Baha, *Abdu'l-Baha in London*: 60-61.

Final Thoughts

1. 'Abdu'l-Baha wrote early last century: "Similarly there are periods and stages in the collective life of humanity. At one time it was passing through its stage of childhood, at another its period of youth, but now it has entered its long-predicted phase of maturity, the evidences of which are everywhere apparent." (Cited by Shoghi Effendi, *The World Order of Baha'u'llah*: 164-165)

2. 'Abdu'l-Baha, *Some Answered Questions*: 79.

3. Universal House of Justice letter dated March 2, 2013.

4. *Selections from the Writings of Abdu'l-Baha*: 275

Bibliography

Abdu'l-Baha, *Abdu'l-Baha in London*. London: Baha'i Publishing Trust, 27 Rutland Gate. 1998.

_____. *Paris Talks*: *Addresses Given by 'Abdu'l-Baha in 1911*. London: Baha'i Publishing Trust, 27 Rutland Gate, 1972.

_____. *The Promulgation of Universal Peace*. Compiled by Howard MacNutt. Wilmette: Baha'i Publishing Trust, 1982.

_____. *The Secret of Divine Civilization*. Wilmette: Baha'i Publishing Trust, 1983.

_____. *Selections from the Writings of 'Abdu'l-Baha*. Trans. by a Committee at the Bahá'í World Centre and by Marzieh Gail. Haifa: Bahá'í World Centre. 1978.

_____. *Some Answered Questions*. Compiled and translated by Laura Clifford Barney. 5th ed. Wilmette: Baha'i Publishing Trust, 1982.

'Abdu'l-Baha, Shoghi Effendi. *Japan Will Turn Ablaze*: Compiled by Barbara Sims. Revised Edition. Tokyo: Bahá'í Publishing Trust. 1992.

Baha'i International Community, 1993 Apr 01, *Sustainable Development and the Human Spirit*.

Baha'i International Community, 1995 October, *Turning Point For All Nations*.

Bahá'í International Community, *Valuing Spirituality in Development:* London: Baha'i Publishing Trust, 27 Rutland Gate. 1998.

Baha'i International Community, 1992 May 29, *Statement on Baha'u'llah*.

Baha'i International Community, 1995, March 03, *The Prosperity of Humankind*. Wilmette: Baha'i Publishing Trust.

Baha'i International Community, 1996 Mar 15, *United Nations Decade for Human Rights Education*.

Bahá'í World Centre. *One Common Faith*. Wilmette: Baha'i Publishing Trust. 2005.

Bahiyyih Khanum: The Greatest Holy Leaf: A compilation from Bahá'í sacred texts and writings of the Guardian of the Faith and Bahiyyih Khanum's own letters Compiled by The Research Department at the Bahá'í World Centre, 1982.

Baha'u'llah, *Epistle to the Son of the Wolf*: Wilmette: Baha'i Publishing Trust. 1976.

Baha'u'llah, The *Summons of the Lord of Hosts*. Wilmette: Baha'i Publishing Trust. 2006.

Baha'u'llah, *The Seven Valleys and The Four Valleys*. Trans. by Ali-Kuli Khan and Marzieh Gail. Wilmette: Baha'i Publishing Trust, 1991.

Baha'u'llah. *Tablets of Baha'u'llah Revealed After the Kitab-i-Aqdas*. Wilmette: Baha'i Publishing Trust. 1978.

Baha'u'llah. *The Hidden Words of Baha'u'llah*. Translated by Shoghi Effendi. Wilmette: Baha'i Publishing Trust. 1985 reprint.

Baha'u'llah. *The Kitab-i-Iqan (The Book of Certitude)*. Translated by Shoghi Effendi. Wilmette: Baha'i Publishing Trust. 1970.

Baha'u'llah. *Gleanings from the Writings of Bahá'u'lláh*. Trans. by Shoghi Effendi. Wilmette: Bahá'í Publishing Trust. 1971.

Baha'u'llah, the Bab, 'Abdu'l-Baha, *Baha'i Prayers: A Selection of Prayers Revealed by Baha'u'llah, the Bab, and 'Abdu'l-Baha*. New ed. Wilmette: Bahá'í Publishing Trust, 1991.

Baha'u'llah, 'Abdu'l-Baha, Shoghi Effendi, and the Universal House of Justice, *The Compilation of Compilations Prepared by the Universal House of Justice*. 2 vols. Maryborough, Victoria: Bahá'í Publishing Trust, 1991.

Barnes, William. *Renewing the Sacred*. Self-published at Createspace. 2012 available from www.Amazon.com or Bahá'í Distribution Services.

Covey, Steven. *Principle-Centered Leadership*. New York. Fireside Books, Simon and Shuster, 1991.

Directives from the Guardian. Compiled by Gertrude Garrida. New Delhi: Bahá'í Publishing Trust, 1973.

Eliade, Mircea. *The Sacred and the Profane: The Nature of Religion*. New York: Harcourt Brace Jovanovich, Inc. 1987.

The Holy Bible, King James translation.

Hornby, Helen. *Lights of Guidance:* A Bahá'í Reference file compiled by Helen Hornby. New Delhi: Bahá'í Publishing Trust. 1994.

Mahmud's Diary: The Diary of Mirza Mahmud-i-Zarqani Chronicling 'Abdu'l-Bahá's Journey to America. Oxford: George Ronald, 1998.

Shoghi Effendi, *Principles of Bahá'í Administration: Selected Messages, 1923-1932*. Wilmette: Baha'i Publishing Trust, 1974.

Shoghi Effendi, *The Advent of Divine Justice*. Wilmette: Baha'i Publishing Trust. 1971.

Shoghi Effendi. *The World Order of Bahá'u'lláh*. Wilmette: Baha'i Publishing Trust. 1991.

Universal House of Justice, *Messages from the Universal House of Justice 1963-1986*. Compiled by Geoffrey W. Marks. Wilmette; Bahá'í Publishing Trust. 1986.

Universal House of Justice. *The Promise of World Peace*. Wilmette: Baha'i Publishing Trust. 1985.

Universal House of Justice. To the Baha'is of the World. *Ridvan 2010*.

Universal House of Justice. To the Baha'is of the World. *Ridvan 2012*.

Universal House of Justice. To the Baha'is of Iran. March 2, 2013.

Universal House of Justice, *To the World's Religious Leaders*. April 2002.

APPENDIX ONE

THE SPIRIT OF JUSTICE

What could be better before God than thinking of the poor? For the poor are beloved by our heavenly Father. When His Holiness Christ came upon the earth those who believed in him and followed him were the poor and lowly, showing the poor were near to God. When a rich man believes and follows the Manifestation of God it is a proof that his wealth is not an obstacle and does not prevent him from attaining the pathway of salvation. After he has been tested and tried it will be seen whether his possessions are a hindrance in his religious life. But the poor are especially beloved of God. Their lives are full of difficulties, their trials continual, their hopes are in God alone. Therefore you must assist the poor as much as possible, even by sacrifice of yourself. No deed of man is greater before God than helping the poor. Spiritual conditions are not dependent upon the possession of worldly treasures or the absence of them. When physically destitute, spiritual thoughts are more likely. Poverty is stimulus toward God. Each one of you must have great consideration for the poor and render them assistance. Organize in an effort to help them and prevent increase of poverty. The greatest means for prevention is that whereby the laws of the community will be so framed and enacted that it will not be possible for a few to be millionaires and many destitute. One of Bahá'u'lláh's teachings is the adjustment of means of livelihood in human society. Under this adjustment there can be no extremes in human conditions as regards wealth and sustenance. For the community needs financier, farmer merchant and laborer just as an army must be composed of commander, officers and privates. All cannot be commanders; all cannot be officers or privates. Each in his station in the social fabric must be competent; each in his function according to ability; but justness of opportunity for all.

Lycurgus, king of Sparta, who lived long before the day of Christ, conceived the idea of absolute equality in government. He proclaimed laws by which all the people of Sparta were classified into certain divisions. Each division had its separate rights and function. First, farmers and tillers of the soil. Second, artisans and merchants. Third, leaders or grandees. Under the laws of Lycurgus the latter were not required to engage in any labor or vocation but it was incumbent upon them to defend the country in case of war and invasion. Then he divided Sparta into nine thousand equal parts or provinces, appointing nine thousand leaders or grandees to protect them. In this way the farmers of each province were assured of protection but each farmer was compelled to pay a tax to support the grandee of that province. The farmers and merchants were not obliged to defend the country. In lieu of labor the grandees received the taxes. Lycurgus in order to establish this forever as a law, brought nine thousand grandees together, told them he was going upon a long journey and wished this form of government to remain effective until his return. They swore an oath to protect and preserve his law. He then left his kingdom, went into voluntary exile and never came back. No man ever made such a sacrifice to insure equality among his fellowmen. A few years passed and the whole system of government he had founded collapsed, although established upon such a just and wise basis.

Difference of capacity in human individuals is fundamental. It is impossible for all to be alike, all to be equal, all to be wise. Bahá'u'lláh has revealed principles and laws which will accomplish the adjustment of varying human capacities. He has said that whatsoever is possible of accomplishment in human government will be effected through these principles. When the laws he has instituted are carried out there will be no millionaires possible in the community and likewise no extremely poor. This will be effected and regulated by adjusting the different degrees of human capacity. The fundamental basis of the community is agriculture, tillage of the soil. All must be producers. Each person in the community whose income is equal to his individual producing capacity shall be exempt from taxation. But if his income is greater than his needs he must pay a tax until an adjustment is effected. That is to say, a man's capacity for production and his needs will be equalized and reconciled through taxation. If his production exceeds he will pay no tax; if his necessities exceed his production he shall receive an amount sufficient to equalize or adjust. Therefore taxation will be proportionate to capacity and production and there will be no poor in the community.

COOPERATION

It seems as though all creatures can exist singly and alone. For example, a tree can exist solitary and alone on a given prairie or in a valley or on the mountainside. An animal upon a mountain or a bird soaring in the air might live a solitary life. They are not in need of cooperation or solidarity. Such animated beings enjoy the greatest comfort and happiness in their respective solitary lives.

On the contrary, man cannot live singly and alone. He is in need of continuous cooperation and mutual help. For example, a man living alone in the wilderness will eventually starve. He can never, singly and alone, provide himself with all the necessities of existence. Therefore, he is in need of cooperation and reciprocity.

The mystery of this phenomenon, the cause thereof is this, that mankind has been created from one single origin, has branched off from one family. Thus in reality all mankind represents one family. God has not created any difference. He has created all as one that thus this family might live in perfect happiness and well-being.

Regarding reciprocity and cooperation: each member of the body politic should live in the utmost comfort and welfare because each individual member of humanity is a member of the body politic and if one member of the members be in distress or be afflicted with some disease all the other members must necessarily suffer. For example, a member of the human organism is the eye. If the eye should be affected that affliction would affect the whole nervous system. Hence, if a member of the body politic becomes afflicted, in reality, from the standpoint of sympathetic connection, all will share that affliction since this (one afflicted) is a member of the group of members, a part of the whole. Is it possible for one member or part to be in distress and the other members to be at ease? It is impossible! Hence God has desired that in the body politic of humanity each one shall enjoy perfect welfare and comfort.

Although the body politic is one family yet because of lack of harmonious relations some members are comfortable and some in direst misery, some members are satisfied and some are hungry, some members are clothed in most costly garments and some families are in need of food and shelter. Why? Because this family lacks the necessary reciprocity and symmetry. This household is not well arranged. This household is not living under a perfect law. All the laws which are legislated do not ensure happiness. They do not provide comfort. Therefore a law must be given to this family by means of which all the members of this family will enjoy equal well-being and happiness.

Is it possible for one member of a family to be subjected to the utmost misery and to abject poverty and for the rest of the family to be comfortable? It is impossible unless those members of the family be senseless, atrophied, inhospitable, unkind. Then they would say, "Though these members do belong to our family—let them alone. Let us look after ourselves. Let them die. So long as I am comfortable, I am honored, I am happy—this my brother—let him die. If he be in misery let him remain in misery, so long as I am comfortable. If he is hungry let him remain so; I am satisfied. If he is without clothes, so long as I am clothed, let him remain as he is. If he is shelterless, homeless, so long as I have a home, let him remain in the wilderness."

Such utter indifference in the human family is due to lack of control, to lack of a working law, to lack of kindness in its midst. If kindness had been shown to the members of this family surely all the members thereof would have enjoyed comfort and happiness.

His Holiness Bahá'u'lláh has given instructions regarding every one of the questions confronting humanity. He has given teachings and instructions with regard to every one of the problems with which man struggles. Among them are (the teachings) concerning the question of economics that all the members of the body politic may enjoy through the working out of this solution the greatest happiness, welfare and comfort without any harm or injury attacking the general order of things. Thereby no difference or dissension will occur. No sedition or contention will take place. This solution is this:

First and foremost is the principle that to all the members of the body politic shall be given the greatest achievements of the world of humanity. Each one shall have the utmost welfare and well-being. To solve this problem we must begin with the farmer; there will we lay a foundation for system and order because the peasant class and the agricultural class exceed other classes in the importance of their service. In every village there must be established a general storehouse which will have a number of revenues.

The first revenue will be that of the tenth or tithes.

The second revenue (will be derived) from the animals.

The third revenue, from the minerals, that is to say, every mine prospected or discovered, a third thereof will go to this vast storehouse.

The fourth is this: whosoever dies without leaving any heirs all his heritage will go to the general storehouse.

Fifth, if any treasures shall be found on the land they should be devoted to this storehouse.

All these revenues will be assembled in this storehouse.

As to the first, the tenths or tithes: we will consider a farmer, one of the peasants. We will look into his income. We will find out, for instance, what is his annual revenue and also what are his expenditures. Now, if his income be equal to his expenditures, from such a farmer nothing whatever will be taken. That is, he will not be subjected to taxation of any sort, needing as he does all his income. Another farmer may have expenses running up to one thousand dollars we will say, and his income is two thousand dollars. From such an one a tenth will be required, because he has a surplus. But if his income be ten thousand dollars and his expenses one thousand dollars or his income twenty thousand dollars, he will have to pay as taxes, one-fourth. If his income be one hundred thousand dollars and his expenses five thousand, one-third will he have to pay because he has still a surplus since his expenses are five thousand and his income one hundred thousand. If he pays, say, thirty-five thousand dollars, in addition to the expenditure of five thousand he still has sixty thousand left. But if his expenses be ten thousand and his income two hundred thousand then he must give an even half because ninety thousand will be in that case the sum remaining. Such a scale as this will determine allotment of taxes. All the income from such revenues will go to this general storehouse.

Then there must be considered such emergencies as follows: a certain farmer whose expenses run up to ten thousand dollars and whose income is only five thousand, he will receive necessary expenses from the storehouse. Five thousand dollars will be allotted to him so he will not be in need.

Then the orphans will be looked after, all of whose expenses will be taken care of. The cripples in the village—all their expenses will be looked after. The poor in the village—their necessary expenses will be defrayed. And other members who for valid reasons are incapacitated—the blind, the old, the deaf—their comfort must be looked after. In the village no one will remain in need or in want. All will live in the utmost comfort and welfare. Yet no schism will assail the general order of the body politic.

Hence the expenses or expenditures of the general storehouse are now made clear and its activities made manifest. The income of this general storehouse has been shown. Certain trustees will be elected by the people in a given village to look after these transactions. The farmers will be taken care of and if after all these expenses are defrayed any surplus is found in the storehouse it must be transferred to the national treasury.

This system is all thus ordered so that in the village the very poor will be comfortable, the orphans will live happily and well; in a word, no one will be left destitute. All the individual members of the body politic will thus live comfortably and well.

For larger cities, naturally, there will be a system on a larger scale. Were I to go into that solution the details thereof would be very lengthy.

The result of this (system) will be that each individual member of the body politic will live most comfortably and happily under obligation to no one. Nevertheless, there will be preservation of degree because in the world of humanity there must needs be degrees. The body politic may well be likened to an army. In this army there must be a general, there must be a sergeant, there must be a marshal, there must be the infantry; but all must enjoy the greatest comfort and welfare.

God is not partial and is no respecter of persons. He has made provision for all. The harvest comes forth for everyone. The rain showers upon everybody and the heat of the sun is destined to warm everyone. The verdure of the earth is for everyone. Therefore there should be for all humanity the utmost happiness, the utmost comfort, the utmost well-being.

But if conditions are such that some are happy and comfortable and some in misery; some are accumulating exorbitant wealth and others are in dire want -- under such a system it is impossible for man to be happy and impossible for him to win the good pleasure of God. God is kind to all. The good pleasure of God consists in the welfare of all the individual members of mankind.

A Persian king was one night in his palace, living in the greatest luxury and comfort. Through excessive joy and gladness he addressed a certain man, saying: "Of all my life this is the happiest moment. Praise be to God, from every point prosperity appears and fortune smiles! My treasury is full and the army is well taken care of. My palaces are many; my land unlimited; my family is well off; my honor and sovereignty are great. What more could I want!"

The poor man at the gate of his palace spoke out, saying: "O kind king! Assuming that you are from every point of view so happy, free from every worry and sadness—do you not worry for us? You say that on your own account you have no worries—but do you never worry about the poor in your land? Is it becoming or meet that you should be so well off and we in such dire want and need? In view of our needs and troubles how can you rest in your palace, how can you even say that you are free from worries and sorrows? As a ruler you must not be so egoistic as to think of yourself alone but you must think of those who are your subjects. When we are comfortable then you will be comfortable; when we are in misery how can you, as a king, be in happiness?"

The purport is this that we are all inhabiting one globe of earth. In reality we are one family and each one of us is a member of this family. We must all be in the greatest happiness and comfort, under a just rule and regulation which is according to the good pleasure of God, thus causing us to be happy, for this life is fleeting.

If man were to care for himself only he would be nothing but an animal for only the animals are thus egoistic. If you bring a thousand sheep to a well to kill nine hundred and ninety-nine the one remaining sheep would go on grazing, not thinking of the others and worrying not at all about the lost, never bothering that its own kind had passed away, or had perished or been killed. To look after one's self only is therefore an animal propensity. It is the animal propensity to live solitary and alone. It is the animal proclivity to look after one's own comfort. But man was created to be a man—to be fair, to be just, to be merciful, to be kind to all his species, never to be willing that he himself be well off while others are in misery and distress—this is an attribute of the animal and not of man. Nay, rather, man should be willing to accept hardships for himself in order that others may enjoy wealth; he should enjoy trouble for himself that others may enjoy happiness and well-being. This is the attribute of man. This is becoming of man. Otherwise man is not man—he is less than the animal.

The man who thinks only of himself and is thoughtless of others is undoubtedly inferior to the animal because the animal is not possessed of the reasoning faculty. The animal is excused; but in man there is reason, the faculty of justice, the faculty of mercifulness. Possessing all these faculties he must not leave them unused. He who is so hard-hearted as to think only of his own comfort, such an one will not be called man.

Man is he who forgets his own interests for the sake of others. His own comfort he forfeits for the well-being of all. Nay, rather, his own life must he be willing to forfeit for the life of mankind. Such a man is the honor of the world of humanity. Such a man is the glory of the world of mankind. Such a man is the one who wins eternal bliss. Such a man is near to the threshold of God. Such a man is the very manifestation of eternal happiness. Otherwise, men are like animals, exhibiting the same proclivities and propensities as the world of animals. What distinction is there? What prerogatives, what perfections? None whatever! Animals are better even—thinking only of themselves and negligent of the needs of others.

Consider how the greatest men in the world—whether among prophets or philosophers—all have forfeited their own comfort, have sacrificed their own pleasure for the well-being of humanity. They have sacrificed their own lives for the body politic. They have sacrificed their own wealth for that of the general welfare. They have forfeited their own honor for the honor of mankind. Therefore it becomes evident that this is the highest attainment for the world of humanity.

We ask God to endow human souls with justice so that they may be fair, and may strive to provide for the comfort of all, that each member of humanity may pass his life in the utmost comfort and welfare. Then this material world will become the very paradise of the Kingdom, this elemental earth will be in a heavenly state and all the servants of God will live in the utmost joy, happiness and gladness. We must all strive and concentrate all our thoughts in order that such happiness may accrue to the world of humanity.

The question of socialization is very important. It will not be solved by strikes for wages. All the governments of the world must be united and organize an assembly the members of which should be elected from the parliaments and the nobles of the nations. These must plan with utmost wisdom and power so that neither the capitalist suffer from enormous losses nor the laborers become needy. In the utmost moderation they should make the law; then announce to the public that the rights of the working people are to be strongly preserved. Also the rights of the capitalists are to be protected. When such a general plan is adopted by the will of both sides, should a strike occur, all the governments of the world collectively should resist it. Otherwise, the labor problem will lead to much destruction, especially in Europe. Terrible things will take place.

For instance, the owners of properties, mines and factories should share their incomes with their employees and give a fairly certain percentage of their products to their workingmen in order that the employees may receive, beside their wages, some of the general income of the factory so that the employee may strive with his soul in the work.

No more trusts will remain in the future. The question of the trusts will be wiped away entirely. Also, every factory that has ten thousand shares will give two thousand shares of these ten thousand to its employees and will write the shares in their names, so that they may have them, and the rest will belong to the capitalists. Then at the end of the month or year whatever they may earn after the expenses and wages are paid, according to the number of shares, should be divided among both. In reality, so far great injustice has befallen the common people. Laws must be made because it is impossible for the laborers to be satisfied with the present system. They will strike every month and every year. Finally, the capitalists will lose. In ancient times a strike occurred among the Turkish soldiers. They said to the government: "Our wages are very small and they should be increased." The government was forced to give them their demands. Shortly afterwards they struck again. Finally all the incomes went to the pockets of the soldiers to the extent that they killed the king, saying: "Why didst thou not increase the income so that we might have received more?"

It is impossible for a country to live properly without laws. To solve this problem rigorous laws must be made, so that all the governments of the world will be the protectors thereof.

In the Bolshevistic principles equality is effected through force. The masses who are opposed to the people of rank and to the wealthy class desire to partake of their advantages.

But in the divine teachings equality is brought about through a ready willingness to share. It is commanded as regards wealth that the rich among the people, and the aristocrats should, by their own free will and for the sake of their own happiness, concern themselves with and care for the poor. This equality is the result of the lofty characteristics and noble attributes of mankind.

(Abdu'l-Baha, *Foundations of World Unity*, p. 34-43)

APPENDIX TWO
Rethinking Prosperity: Forging Alternatives to a Culture of Consumerism

Baha'i International Community's Contribution to the 18th Session of the United Nations Commission on Sustainable Development

3 May 2010
New York

Against the backdrop of climate change, environmental degradation, and the crippling extremes of wealth and poverty, the transformation from a culture of unfettered consumerism to a culture of sustainability has gained momentum in large part through the efforts of civil society organizations and governmental agencies worldwide. Beyond informed policies and 'greener technologies' it is a transformation that will require an earnest examination of our understanding of human nature and of the cultural frameworks driving institutions of government, business, education, and media around the world. Questions of what is natural and just will need to be critically re-examined. The issue of sustainable consumption and production, under consideration by this Commission, will need to be considered in the broader context of an ailing social order—one characterized by competition, violence, conflict and insecurity—of which it is a part.

In its contribution to the Commissions' review of the 10-Year Framework for Programmes on sustainable consumption and production, the Baha'i International Community would like, first, to note the strengths of this evolving Framework and, second—in line with the vision outlined above—to identify issues which require further elaboration. In terms of its strengths: the Framework considers the economic, social and environmental aspects of the transition to sustainable consumption and production, thereby breaking down the long-standing compartmentalization of these domains; it recognizes the inter-linkages between the themes of the Framework (e.g. education, institutional capacity building, participation of women, application of indigenous knowledge, etc.); it has sought to involve stakeholders from around the world through regional consultations; and it calls on actors from all levels of society to achieve the goals articulated therein.

Yet, given that the Framework seeks to promote the shift towards sustainable consumption and production—implicitly challenging cultural norms and values, which have promoted consumerism at all cost—a number of underlying conceptions will need to be examined and, in many cases, revised in order to advance the goals therein. These include conceptions of human nature; of development (and the nature of progress and prosperity); of the nature and causes of recent economic crises; of processes of technological development; and of the means and ends of educational processes. We invite others actively working to promote sustainable consumption and production to engage with us in dialogue about these underlying issues in order to learn from each other's perspectives and experiences and to collectively advance efforts to build a just and sustainable society.

Human nature

The question of human nature has an important place in the discourse on sustainable consumption and production as it prompts us to reexamine, at the deepest levels, who we are and what our purpose is in life. The human experience is essentially spiritual in nature: it is rooted in the inner reality—or what some call the 'soul'—that we all share in common. The culture of consumerism, however, has tended to reduce human beings to competitive, insatiable consumers of goods and to objects of manipulation by the market. Commonly held views have assumed the existence of an intractable conflict between what people really want (i.e. to consume more) and what humanity needs (i.e. equitable access to resources). How, then, can we resolve the paralyzing contradiction that, on the one hand, we desire a world of peace and prosperity, while, on the other, much of economic and psychological theory depicts human beings as slaves to self-interest? The faculties needed to construct a more just and sustainable social order—moderation, justice, love, reason, sacrifice and service to the common good—have too often been dismissed as naïve ideals. Yet, it is these, and related, qualities that must be harnessed to overcome the traits of ego, greed, apathy and violence, which are often rewarded by the market and political forces driving current patterns of unsustainable consumption and production.

Vision of development

In a similar manner, the articulation of a vision of sustainability must emerge from a public discourse on the nature and purpose of human development and the roles assigned to its protagonists.

The Baha'i International Community understands the transition to sustainable consumption and production as part of a global enterprise which enables all individuals to fulfill their dual purpose, namely to develop their inherent potentialities and to contribute to the betterment of the wider community. It is not enough to conceive of sustainable consumption and production in terms of creating opportunities for those living in poverty to meet their basic needs. Rather, with the understanding that each individual has a contribution to make to the construction of a more just and peaceful social order, these processes must be arranged in a way that permits each to play his or her rightful role as productive member of society. Within such a framework, sustainable consumption and production could be characterized as processes that provide for the material, social and spiritual needs of humanity across generations and enable all peoples to contribute to the ongoing advancement of society.

Progress at the technical and policy levels now needs to be accompanied by public dialogue—among rural and urban dwellers; among the materially poor and the affluent; among men, women and young persons alike—on the ethical foundations of the necessary systemic change. A sustainable social order is distinguished, among other things, by an ethic of reciprocity and balance at all levels of human organization. A relevant analogy is the human body: here, millions of cells collaborate to make human life possible. The astounding diversity of form and function connects them in a lifelong process of giving and receiving. It represents the highest expression of unity in diversity. Within such an order, the concept of justice is embodied in the recognition that the interests of the individual and of the wider community are inextricably linked. The pursuit of justice within the frame of unity (in diversity) provides a guide for collective deliberation and decision-making and offers a means by which unified thought and action can be achieved.

Ultimately, the transformation required to shift towards sustainable consumption and production will entail no less than an organic change in the structure of society itself so as to reflect fully the interdependence of the entire social body—as well as the interconnectedness with the natural world that sustains it. Among these changes, many of which are already the focus of considerable public discourse, are: the consciousness of world citizenship; the eventual federation of all nations through an integrated system of governance with capacity for global decision-making; the establishment of structures which recognize humanity's common ownership of the earth's resources; the establishment of full equality between men and women; the elimination of all forms of prejudice; the establishment of a universal currency and other integrating mechanisms that promote global economic justice; the adoption of an international auxiliary language to facilitate mutual understanding; and the redirection of massive military expenditures towards constructive social ends.

Crisis in the current economic system

As is well known, the dominant model of development depends on a society of vigorous consumers of material goods. In such a model, endlessly rising levels of consumption are cast as indicators of progress and prosperity. This preoccupation with the production and accumulation of material objects and comforts (as sources of meaning, happiness and social acceptance) has consolidated itself in the structures of power and information to the exclusion of competing voices and paradigms. The unfettered cultivation of needs and wants has led to a system fully dependent on excessive consumption for a privileged few, while reinforcing exclusion, poverty and inequality, for the majority. Each successive global crisis—be it climate, energy, food, water, disease, financial collapse—has revealed new dimensions of the exploitation and oppression inherent in the current patterns of consumption and production. Stark are the contrasts between the consumption of luxuries and the cost of provision of basic needs: basic education for all would cost $10 billion; yet $82 billion is spent annually on cigarettes in the United States alone. The eradication of world hunger would cost $30 billion; water and sanitation—$10 billion. By comparison, the world's military budget rose to $1.55 trillion in 2008.

The narrowly materialistic worldview underpinning much of modern economic thinking has contributed to the degradation of human conduct, the disruption of families and communities, the corruption of public institutions, and the exploitation and marginalization of large segments of the population—women and girls in particular. Unarguably, economic activity and the strengthening of the economy (a process that may include, but is not synonymous with, economic growth) have a central role to play in achieving the prosperity of a region and its people. Yet the shift towards a more just, peaceful and sustainable society will require attention to a harmonious dynamic between the material and non-material (or moral) dimensions of consumption and production. The latter, in particular, will be essential for laying the foundation for just and peaceful human relations; these include the generation of knowledge, the cultivation of trust and trustworthiness, eradication of racism and violence, promotion of art, beauty, science, and the capacity for collaboration and the peaceful resolution of conflicts.

In this light, it is also important to emphasize the relationship between production and employment as a critical dimension of a strong economy. Too often, increases in productivity have been accompanied by delocalization or a transition to automation and thus, rising levels of unemployment. A single-minded focus on profit-maximization has also valued workforce reduction wherever possible. Under the present system, unemployment and underemployment are soaring and the majority of the world's population does not earn enough to meet their basic needs. Those living in poverty have no means by which to express themselves in such a system. Sustainable production is not simply about 'greener' technology but rather, should involve systems that enable all human beings to contribute to the productive process. In such a system, all are producers, and all have the opportunity to earn (or receive, if unable to earn) enough to meet their needs. More than simply the means of generating wealth and meeting basic needs, work provides a role in the community and developing one's talents, refining one's character, rendering service and contributing to the advancement of society.

Technological development

The Framework for Programmes highlights the importance of technology transfer and knowledge sharing for achieving sustainable levels of consumption and production. Yet, the majority of technological development is driven by market forces that do not reflect the basic needs of the world's peoples. Furthermore, the emphasis on the transfer of technology without accompanying efforts to increase participation in the generation and application of knowledge can only serve to widen the gap between the rich and the poor—the 'developers' and the 'users' of technology. Developing the capacity for identifying technological need and for technological innovation and adaptation—in light of societal needs and environmental constraints—will be vital to social progress. The transformation of complex social realities will require the development of institutional capacity within local populations to create and apply knowledge in ways that address the specific needs of that population. This question of institutional capacity (e.g. the establishment of regional centers of research and training) constitutes a major challenge to sustainable development. If successfully met, however, the result will be to break the present unbalanced flow of knowledge in the world and dissociate development from ill-conceived processes of modernization. "Modern" technologies will be characterized by an orientation towards addressing locally defined needs and by priorities that take into account both the material and moral prosperity of society as a whole.

Education

The Framework for Programmes identifies education and institutional capacity building as two of the programs that could support the implementation of sustainable patterns of consumption and production. Yet, if they are to effect the profound changes in the minds of people and in the structures of society (needed to shift towards sustainability), the nature of the educational processes will need to be rethought. As a starting point, the program of education must be based on a clear vision of the kind of society that we wish to live in; and the kind of individuals that will bring this about. It needs to help learners reflect on the purpose of life and help them to step out of their cultural realities to develop alternative visions and approaches to the problems at hand and to understand the manifold consequences of their behaviors and to adjust these accordingly.

Schools themselves must become participants in the social transformation processes. The curriculum cannot simply aim to impart relevant knowledge and skills; rather it should aim to develop the vast potential inherent in the human being. Individuals must be assisted to channel this potential towards the betterment of their communities and the advancement of society as a whole. The level of consciousness and the deep spirit of service and collaboration required to transform individual behaviors and institutional forces in the direction of sustainability will require a transformation of educational processes commensurate with the task at hand.

Baha'i community's approach to cultural transformation

Cultural transformation involves deliberate changes in individual choices and in institutional structures and norms. For over a decade, the worldwide Baha'i community has been endeavoring systematically to effect a transformation among individuals and communities around the world—to inspire and build the capacity for service. The framework for action guiding these activities has been rooted in a dynamic of learning—characterized by action, reflection, and consultation. In thousands of communities, Baha'is have set into motion neighborhood-level processes that seek to empower individuals of all ages to recognize and develop their spiritual capacities and to channel their collective energies towards the betterment of their communities. Aware of the aspirations of the children of the world and their need for spiritual education, they have started children's classes that focus on laying the foundations of a noble and upright character. For youth aged 11-14, they have created a learning environment which helps them to form their moral identity at this critical time in their life and to develop skills which empower them to channel their constructive and creative energies toward the betterment of their communities. All are invited to take part in small groups of participatory learning around core concepts and themes which encourage individuals to become agents of change in their communities within a dynamic of learning and an orientation towards service.

The approach to curriculum development for these activities has not been one of design, field testing and evaluation; rather the first step in writing any set of materials has been taken when experience emerges from grassroots action in response to particular development needs. Curriculum materials are continually refined in light of new knowledge and insights. The cultural shifts taking place are evident in the greater capacity to carry out collective action, to see oneself as an agent of change in the community, as a humble learner, as an active participant in the generation, diffusion and application of knowledge. The continuous cycle of learning through action, reflection and consultation has raised awareness of the needs and resources across communities as well as strengthened the mechanisms for collective action and deliberation.

In addition, professionals in various fields have joined together in organizations inspired by Baha'i principles and values to work for sustainable consumption and production. The European Baha'i Business Forum and affiliated bodies in other regions are working with business leaders to consider social purposes beyond profit, including sustainability in production processes and corporate responsibility. The International Environment Forum has long promoted sustainable lifestyles and more ethical consumption, including participation in the former Consumer Citizenship Network in Europe and now the Partnership for Education and Research for Responsible Living.

The movement to redefine cultural norms in light of the exigencies of justice and sustainability is well underway. In different measures, leading cultural institutions, including governments, education and media, as well as businesses, religious organizations and civil society are bringing the values of sustainability to the forefront of public consciousness. Broader visions of human purpose and prosperity are moving from the periphery to the center of public discourse. It is becoming clear that the pathway to sustainability will be one of empowerment, collaboration and continual processes of questioning, learning and action in all regions of the world. It will be shaped by the experiences of women, men, children, the rich, the poor, the governors and the governed as each one is enabled to play their rightful role in the construction of a new society. As the sweeping tides of consumerism, unfettered consumption, extreme poverty and marginalization recede, they will reveal the human capacities for justice, reciprocity and happiness.

---

1. The main objective of the 10-Year Framework for Programmes is to be a global framework for action on sustainable consumption and production (SCP) that countries can endorse and commit to in order to accelerate the shift towards sustainable consumption and production patterns, thereby promoting social and economic development within the carrying capacity of ecosystems and de-linking economic growth from environmental degradation. The main challenge is to provide not only the key programs of the framework, but also the mechanisms for their implementation (e.g. financial support, capacity building, and technical assistance). See: Proposed Input to CSD 18 and 19 on a 10 Year Framework of Programmes on Sustainable Consumption and Production. Third Public Draft (2 September 2009). Prepared by the Marrakech Process Secretariat: UN Department of Economic and Social Affairs (UNDESA) and UN Environment Programme(UNEP).
[http://esa.un.org/marrakechprocess/pdf/Draft3_10yfpniputtoCSD2Sep09.pdf]

2. "Applying a Life-Cycle Perspective to the economic system can provide a way to structure the overall approach of the

10YFP as well as identify clear entry points for actions as well as actors. It allows for single focus on either production or consumption, or integrated focus on both while taking into account the economic, social and environmental impacts of products and services throughout their whole life-cycle. Because it is based on the total use of resources going into the production of goods and provision of services as well as the resulting emissions and waste, this life-cycle perspective provides a holistic picture of all the entry points for remediation as well as possible synergistic intervention throughout the production and consumption chain." Proposed Input to CSD 18 and 19 on a 10 Year Framework of Programmes (see Note 1).

3. Ibid.

4. "The enormous energy dissipated and wasted on war, whether economic or political, will be consecrated to such ends as will extend the range of human inventions and technical development, to the increase of the productivity of mankind, to the extermination of disease, to the extension of scientific research, to the raising of the standard of physical health, to the sharpening and refinement of the human brain, to the exploitation of the unused and unsuspected resources of the planet, to the prolongation of human life, and to the furtherance of any other agency that can stimulate the intellectual, the moral, and spiritual life of the entire human race." Shoghi Effendi, The World Order of Baha'u'llah (Wilmette: Baha'i Publishing Trust, 1991). (http://reference.bahai.org/en/t/se/WOB/wob-56.html).

5. According to the Worldwatch Institute, consumption expenditures per person almost tripled between 1960 and 2006. (Worldwatch Institute, State of the World 201: The Rise and Fall of Consumer Cultures. New York: W.W. Norton & Company, 2010.) 60 billion tons of resources are extracted

annually—50 percent more than 30 years ago. (Tim Jackson, Prosperity without growth? The transition to a sustainable economy. London: Sustainable Development Commission. March 2009;
http://www.sd-commission.org.uk/publications/downloads/prosperity_without_growth_report.pdf). The 2005 Millennium Ecosystem Assessment found that some 60% of ecosystem services—climate regulation, the provision of fresh water, waste treatment, food from fisheries, etc.—were being degraded or used unsustainably. (Millennium Ecosystem Assessment,
Ecosystems and Human Well-Being: Synthesis. Washington, DC: Island Press, 2005.)

6. Action Aid (United Kingdom). Fact File.
(http://www.actionaid.org.uk). See also: Sperling, Gene B. (Director of the Center for Universal Education, USA). The Case for Universal Basic Education for the World's Poorest Boys and Girls. November 2005. (Council on Foreign Relations, www.cfr.org).

7. The Case for Center for Disease Control and Prevention. Economic Facts About U.S. Tobacco Use and Tobacco Production. (Cites 2005 data).
[http://www.cdc.gov/tobacco/data_statistics/fact_sheets/economics/econ_fa....

8. United Nations. Press Release. Secretary-General Calls for $30 Billion to Restructure World Agriculture, Create Long-Term Food Security. 30 November 2008.
[http://www.un.org/esa/ffd/doha/press/foodsideevent.pdf]

9. "The estimated cost of closing the gap between current trends and what is needed to meet the target ranges from $10billion to $18 billion per year." United Nations Department of Public Information. Press Release. Secretary-General,

addressing side event, spells out areas 'crying out for action' to advance implementation of water and sanitation agenda. 25 September 2008.
[http://www.un.org/News/Press/docs/2008/sgsm11813.doc.htm].
10. International Institute for Strategic Studies.
[http://www.iiss.org/whats-new/iiss-in-the-press/february-2010/report-mil...

11. Just as the physical body possesses physical capacities for movement, growth, etc., so too the soul has capacities, which can be consciously developed. These capacities include human consciousness; the power of intellect and rational thought; the capacity to love; the power of will; and the capacity to initiate and sustain action for the betterment of society, to name a few.

12. International Environment Forum: www.iefworld.org

13. Partnership for Education and Research about Responsible Living:http://www.hihm.no/hihm/Prosjektsider/CCN/PERL

www.ingramcontent.com/pod-product-compliance
Lightning Source LLC
Chambersburg PA
CBHW051809170526
45167CB00005B/1936